"Oscar Miro-Quesada, my dear friend of over thirty years, is both a Western-educated psychologist and traditionally initiated shaman. His book, *Lessons in Courage*, is a profound, articulate, and gripping account of Oscar's deep-rooted apprenticeship with don Celso Rojas, a renowned *curandero* from Salas, Peru. Oscar is a true genius, a genuinely warm and loving individual, and these qualities shine through in the book. A compelling tale about our human quest for wholeness, *Lessons in Courage* openly chronicles Oscar's befriending of sacred and profane dimensions of life, giving us a brilliant rendition of the uncompromising light so often encountered at the end of the tunnel."

—Raymond Moody, MD, PhD, author of *Life After Life*

"This is a great book that can attune the worlds of indigenous peoples with the rational scientific traditions of the modern world. It guides us toward incarnation of all levels of ourselves. Oscar embodies this wholeness and reveals the processes learned in his own epic journey through fields of reality from the Earth to the Star people, from contemporary academic knowledge to the depth and power of indigenous wisdom and ritual, most especially the Pachakuti Mesa Tradition of cross-cultural shamanism. "Lessons in Courage" is an indispensable classic for our *"generation one,"* everyone on the planet, facing for the first time the evolution or devolution of Earth life by our own actions."

—Barbara Marx Hubbard, *Foundation for Conscious Evolution*

"A fascinating inside view of the *mesa* spiritual tradition by a leading Peruvian practitioner written in collaboration with an initiated anthropologist."

—Michael Harner, Ph.D., author of *Cave and Cosmos: Shamanic Encounters with Another Reality* and *The Way of the Shaman*

LESSONS
in
COURAGE

Peruvian Shamanic
Wisdom for Everyday Life

Bonnie Glass-Coffin, Ph.D. *and*
don Oscar Miro-Quesada

RAINBOW RIDGE
BOOKS

Cover and interior design by Frame25 Productions
Cover photo © ollirg c/o Shutterstock.com

Published by:
Rainbow Ridge Books, LLC
140 Rainbow Ridge Road
Faber, Virginia 22938
434-361-1723

If you are unable to order this book from your local bookseller, you may order directly from the distributor.

Square One Publishers, Inc.
115 Herricks Road
Garden City Park, NY 11040
Phone: (516) 535-2010
Fax: (516) 535-2014
Toll-free: 877-900-BOOK

Visit the authors at:
www.mesaworks.com and *www.heartofthehealer.org*

Library of Congress Cataloging-in-Publication Data applied for.

ISBN 978-1-937907-18-1

10 9 8 7 6 5 4 3

Printed on acid-free recycled paper in the United States of America

CONTENTS

PROLOGUE

I first met don Oscar Miro-Quesada in 2005, at the 5th
Annual International Gathering of the Heart of the Healer
Foundation. Don Oscar founded this non-profit service organization (www.heartofthehealer.org), with the vision that it
might serve as an umbrella for teaching shamanic healing arts
and preserving indigenous earth-honoring wisdom traditions.
I had been invited to speak at that year's gathering, held at
a church camp on the shores of Lake Michigan, because of
my own history studying Peruvian shamanism. As an anthropologist, I had been living and working in Peru on and off
since 1975. I had completed my dissertation working with
female shamans on the north coast of Peru. I had written a
book and published many articles about the magic and mystery of *curanderismo* as it is practiced there. In that context,
shamanic healers use ground altars called *mesas* to restore their
patients to health by calling on their spirit allies—from every
kingdom of nature—to assist. Through a ceremonial process
that involves song and spoken prayer, offerings of sound and
scent, pattern and color, these helping spirits fly from every
corner of nature to inhabit the medicine pieces (called *artes*)
that stand upon these altars. In my years studying shamanism
on the north coast of Peru, I had witnessed many miracles of

healing during these shamanic rituals. But, until meeting don Oscar, I never understood how it happens, nor had I been touched by the magic myself.

This gathering was the first time I saw a version of these altars in a North American context. In a beautiful, enclosed gazebo just up the hill from the large hall where the main events of the weekend were taking place, eight of his most advanced students had been asked to set up their own mesas. These radiated out like spokes from a central altar in the middle of the room. When I walked in, the aesthetic beauty of what I saw just overwhelmed me. The aroma of fragrant incense filled the space, its smoke wafting skyward toward the open-beamed ceiling. At each end of the sun-bathed room sat an attendant, one male and one female, in lotus position— both with blissful looks in their eyes. *Artes* were placed on each of the eight mesas, and although each mesa contained different objects, they were all laid out similarly, in mandala-like shapes, with perfect symmetry and grace. The feathers and flowers, crystals and smooth stones, conch shells and candles, framed photos and small statues that were set upon the ground cloths made me think of the slightly wild beauty of an English garden. Each piece just seemed to grow right out of the ground cloth on which it sat. As I walked respectfully around the outside of this gigantic three-dimensional patchwork quilt, I felt myself stepping more buoyantly. My heart grew warm, and I began to smile as I soaked in the beauty before me. This was my first exposure to the "Pachakuti Mesa Tradition," as don Oscar referred to it, and I was enchanted.

Back in the great hall, I delivered my remarks, and then I listened to don Oscar speak. He shared a message about how to live in harmony and respect with our Earth mother and with one another. What was needed, he insisted, was a return to a more respectful way of living—which was founded in the notion that we are all related and that we get what we give. Over the course of the weekend, all those gathered listened to these wisdoms in the great hall. We built sacred fires and shared prayers of gratitude to the great waters of the lake. As the weekend progressed, we also shared stories and broke bread together, and we began calling one another "brother" and "sister." The days were warm, and as time passed, I found myself shedding layers of disdain and hopelessness, cynicism and loneliness, just as naturally as I was shedding my shoes. I found it easier and easier to smile. As I looked around the great hall whenever we gathered, I saw in the faces of all present the same openness that I was feeling. I began to picture each person gathered there as "family."

The night before the last day of the gathering, I remember feeling completely dejected that this event was ending. Like the proverbial kid who revels in the attentions received at her first birthday party only to find herself alone again when the party is over, a deep yearning for connection had been awakened somewhere deep inside of me. Although not religious, I remember uttering a desperate prayer as I dropped off to sleep that I might find a sense of meaning and belonging—somehow. And in my dreams that night, don Oscar appeared. I remember him looking deep into my eyes. I remember his smile. He said, "If you are sincere in your desire, and if you are truly open to change, when you awake in the morning, you will begin to find what you seek."

Six months later, this extraordinary man invited me to his home in South Florida. Armed with a book proposal and a sabbatical project idea, I told him that I had been so touched by what I had experienced at Lake Michigan that I wanted to write a story about transformation. He listened intently as I explained. First, I wanted to explore how the shamanic healing traditions of north coastal Peru that I had studied had been transformed as he had brought this tradition north to the United States. I also wanted to explore how his life had changed in the process of his own apprenticeships. Additionally, I wanted to know about transformation in the lives of the students who had studied the Pachakuti Mesa Tradition with him. Finally, I wanted to explore how anthropology as a discipline might transform through the kind of experimental writing that I hoped to do. After I finished pitching my proposal to him, he looked me deeply in the eyes, just as he had in my dream six months before, and he said simply, "Of course I'm willing to help you write your ethnography of transformation. But before I do, tell me this: Are you first willing to be transformed?"

Thus began my own journey of transformation. It was, as don Oscar is fond of saying, a long journey, because it involved that seventeen-inch transit from head to heart. In the seven years since that invitation, I have immersed myself completely in my own processes of awakening. I have apprenticed deeply to don Oscar's teachings through attendance at weekend workshops and intensive trainings. I participated in a three-year apprenticeship in bio-energetic healing and have been endorsed as a teacher of the Pachakuti Mesa Tradition. I have volunteered in many positions with the Heart of the Healer Foundation.

When don Oscar asked me to help him to put some of his transformational life story and some of his teachings into writing in the summer of 2012, I was deeply touched and honored because, until that time, he had mainly shared these stories, teachings, and traditions orally, according to the wishes of his first shamanic teacher. Yet we were approaching December 21, 2012, (and the beginning of all the prophesied transformations signified by its arrival). Don Oscar knew it was time to put some of his life story on paper to assist us. I am deeply honored to craft the manuscript that can assist him in this task.

Don Oscar's story is one of great courage. It is also a story that carries with it a great message. It is the story of a young man who awakened to his own beauty and wholeness while facing the same kinds of life challenges that test us all: we all struggle to find ourselves, to find meaning in our lives, and to recognize our greater purpose, which is to serve others. His story shows us the way.

Born in Lima in 1951 to a very intellectual family, Oscar Miro-Quesada spent his early years in Peru. As a child, he struggled with chronic illness, he struggled in school, and he struggled with family dysfunction. When he was ten, he experienced what many would describe as a miraculous healing facilitated by beings from "beyond the veil." This experience informed his early interest in exploring shamanism as a doorway into all the realms of consciousness that can help us understand life's deeper mysteries.

More "Spanish" than "Indian" by Peruvian standards, he felt as though he was a "stranger in a strange land." When he was seventeen, he began to *awaken* to his connection with a heritage that is much deeper than simply biological. It is the heritage of the 3,000-year-old shamanic tradition practiced by his ancestors. This book presents the legacy of his heritage, which holds the promise for restoring us to right relationship with ourselves, with one another, and with our beloved Mother Earth.

Between age seventeen and age thirty-one, don Oscar split his time between the north coast of Peru, where he apprenticed with his cherished shamanic teacher don Celso Rojas Palomino, and the United States, where he completed college, graduate, and post-graduate studies. After returning to Peru in 1982, he began a new apprenticeship with don Benito Corihuaman Vargas. After don Benito's passing, he came again to the United States to fulfill his original promise to don Celso to "bring the teachings north." It was in that year that he began teaching the shamanic practices that are the focus of this book. Since 1986, he has taught tens of thousands of students, established a framework for the emergence of a global shamanic community based on the principle that "right action, borne of compassionate spiritual wisdom, unites" and founded the Heart of the Healer Foundation (THOTH), which continues to expand the legacy of these soul-enriching wisdom teachings today.

In the seven years since this project began, I have been blessed and deeply touched by don Oscar's shamanic teachings as well as his close friendship. These experiences also helped us in our work as co-authors. The project has been a seamless and joyful co-creation. I have created the overarching structure for the presentation of don Oscar's life and teachings (for which I take complete responsibility, especially where this framing falls short of truly communicating the beauty inherent in the message). But it is the one-on-one interviews I conducted with don Oscar as well as more than 600 pages of materials gathered from notes compiled during teachings and trainings that allows his own voice, as the sole author of his life's journey, to shine through. I am honored by the trust he has placed in me now to render some of his transformational life story and his teachings on paper. My fervent hope is that I may thus be of some service as both a quill and a vessel for the message. May the great scribe Thoth speak through my heart as I write.

In addition to my deepest debt to don Oscar Miro-Quesada, I am full to overflowing with gratitude to all teachers of the seen and unseen worlds who have supported this adventure. There are too many "two-leggeds" in the *ayllus* and *suyus* of my Pachakuti Mesa Tradition family to thank individually here, yet I trust you know who you are and how much I love you all. I would be remiss, though, not to mention Jason Blaesing and Matt Magee, whose friendship and whose books about the practices and the cosmological background that inform the Pachakuti Mesa Tradition have lifted me up. To Poetic Panther for providing her transcriptions of tapes from don Oscar's teachings of the early 1990s, to Anita Stewart, whose words I have largely borrowed for the *despacho* practice described at the close of chapter 5, to Bonnie Knezo for holding the vision of this completed story and to Cindy Miro-Quesada for her mastery of all the worlds, I also offer my most heartfelt thanks. Pachis, pachis, pachis . . . for all my relations.

Bonnie Glass-Coffin, Ph.D.
Logan, Utah/March 2013

INTRODUCTION

I am Oscar Manuel Miro-Quesada and this is my story. It is a story told within the immediacy of the present moment, even as it recalls the past. It is a story about how I came to serve the earth by returning to the origins of a once-forgotten tradition. It is a story about how honoring these ancient wisdoms can awaken us all to the spiritual dimensions of life.

Some people say that my story is extraordinary, yet, apart from the particularities of my journey, it is a story that we all share. Like me, you have suffered. Like me, you have the power to choose in every moment to awaken to the lessons before you. Your soul, just like mine, is evolving toward great mastery. Like me, you are also a native child of Mother Earth, indigenous to our planet. Like me, you can either choose to be a victim or an evolutionary partner in the unfolding of the great sacred hoop of life. My fondest dream is that you shall volunteer for the latter.

As I share my particular journey with you now, my wish is that you *remember* to receive life as it is, in order to embrace the wholeness of your birthright. Remembering used to be easier than it is now. Once upon a time, we moved through a wilderness where every plant, every rock, and every animal spoke to us, each embracing us in its song. Every moment was animated, charged with vitality and a sense of life-affirming wonder. All humanity delighted in the ebb and flow of this fluid correspondence with the natural world. When we were attentive and appreciative, we remained immersed in the abundant spirit of Mother Nature. We viscerally understood our Earth mother's personal dream. We were aware of the diverse expressions of her cosmic eras and world cycles. Sensitive to the seen and unseen forces that held the fabric of creation together, we established deep alliances with those powers for the greatest good of all.

In that time, we kept alive the ritual honoring of the seasons, the songs, dances, sacred pilgrimages, and the community living needed to cultivate this respectful relationship. Our children became elders who shared with every new generation the wisdom of these courtesies. The earth and humanity continued to peacefully co-exist in sacred trust.

We all carry a template that remembers. But with the rise of the modern world, it has been so easy to forget the truth of sacred relationship. We have fallen into a long and painful sleep of forgetfulness as we have become isolated from one another—and from our true selves. In forgetting, we suffer the physical, emotional, and spiritual pain of separation and of loss. Yet this suffering is often the driving force that allows us to attend again to what is really a call from the true self. These difficult experiences can help us to awaken and to remember. The story I tell here is how I came to this place of remembering my beauty—and my wholeness. My prayer is that it may serve you on your journey also.

I have waited many, many years to share these words. I have waited to write this book because the wisdoms of my teachers are part of an oral tradition that flows like water from the mountains of my homeland. To keep it flowing, changing—ever evolving—through an oral transmission was my first teacher's deepest desire. However, I find myself compelled to share my story in this moment because the time of the great "world-turning" called the *pachakuti* that was prophesied by my ancestors is upon us. In this time of great challenge, I feel an urgency to share these teachings in a way that can reach beyond the sound of my voice.

The wisdoms I share here will help comfort and save us because they give us hope, courage, and the tools to change. They affirm that we *do* have the power to create a New Earth in the midst of a seemingly crumbling world. With these wisdoms, we remember that we are powerful, whole, and *at one* with the Great Originating Mystery. We recognize that all separation, all feeling of being cut-off from the Creator, all feeling of "dismemberment" is illusion. We *re-member* who we are. And as we *re-member,* we will once again live authentic lives of service as we reclaim our place in the unfolding story. We *are* the ones we have been waiting for. And it all begins with the individual soul.

Many have asked the question, "What is Soul?" If you ask me, I will tell you this: soul is alchemy, transformation—ever-changing evolution. It is multiple experiences of being—over the course of our lives and over lifetimes.

The soul's evolution is the focus of this book. As we learn to offer gratitude to the unseen world, perform graceful rituals and heartfelt ceremony, and call upon the ancestral wisdoms of Earth's original peoples, we return to the Garden, to be *at one* with the Source from which all creation flows. This return to wholeness unleashes in us the power to change the world.

The particular rituals that my teachers shared with me derive from the north coastal and central Andean regions of Peru. They include the ritual creation and management of a *mesa* or healing altar in ways that allow the forces and powers of nature to flow through. As these powers are managed, wholeness and transpersonal harmony is restored, both within ourselves and throughout our beloved Mother Earth.

As these rituals begin to be practiced, earth-honoring sacred communities come together again for a common purpose. With this coming together, there is a quickening and a morphic resonance that is created. Healing happens more quickly as a result.

As a fellow traveler on this path, I know that in order to transform ourselves, we must first respond to life's challenges. We are on an adventure that leads us to embrace our innermost feelings and fears. It is a journey of courage and of return to an awareness of our beauty and purpose. This is how the soul evolves. Mastery of these challenges, like all good art, requires human creativity and disciplined imagination. It requires great courage as well. Thus, each of the chapters in this book presents a challenge that we must face, as well as the tools and the wisdoms to move forward.

The name of the great Egyptian scribe Thoth serves as a fitting acronym to present these challenges, for mastering these is an alchemical process. As we successfully move through this process, we unlock the Divine within ourselves. We are like Thoth also because our willingness to play this sacred game of soul-evolution transforms us into sacred messengers to others. We become, through our apprenticeship to life's mysteries, participants in an ever-expanding global shamanic community at a most auspicious time. In THOTH, or **T**rusting Soul,

Honoring Spirit, **O**pening Heart, **T**ransforming Mind, and **H**ealing Body, we awaken to our true selves as we reclaim our birthright of unlimited power to change the world.

Each of the chapters in this small text presents one of these mysteries, which have all been encoded into the Pachakuti Mesa itself. Each chapter begins with a challenge, followed by pieces of my life story to show how these issues have manifested themselves for me. After that, I share insights that have come from my journey. These are highly condensed versions of teachings I offer my students in workshops and trainings. Then, I offer a few practices for daily living that draw from the Pachakuti Mesa Tradition as tools for addressing these fundamental challenges in our lives.

My deepest desire is that the words in this little text may serve you in your journey even as you carry their message of personal and planetary transformation to others. For, even as these teachings are needed *now*, they must also be carried forward as graceful rituals, befitting of the next seven generations. It is my wish that you receive these words as both a charge and a comfort. This is my sacred bequest to you.

The Bequest

It was a gloomy, overcast day in 1981 as I was traveling north from Lima to see don Celso. Since our first encounter in 1969, he had been my *maestro*—mentor, teacher, and way-shower. Don Celso Rojas Palomino had initiated me into the secrets of a 3000-year-old shamanic tradition called *kamasqa curanderismo*. He had opened me to the world of my ancestors.

As I pondered the rumors that had propelled me to visit this time, my mind wandered back to our first meeting. "I have been waiting for you, my son," don Celso had told me, as he raised his eyebrows in surprise at the three surfing buddies who stood with me in his dirt-packed yard.

It was a Tuesday afternoon just before my eighteenth birthday. With our surfboards and a spirit of adventure, we four had traveled to the north coast in order to find this famed *huachumero*. We wanted to drink the visionary San Pedro plant-medicine for which he was known. As he spoke softly, his dark eyes revealed generations of both magic and mystery. As I looked deep within them, they also reflected who he knew me to be. It was a moment of instant, mutual recognition. He soon sent my three buddies packing and welcomed me to stay and change my life.

Outside my car window, a landscape of stark contrasts now stretched before me. Bone-dry deserts punctuated by wide green ribbons caught my gaze. Wherever the earth was touched by life-giving rivers that flow down from the mountains, fields of sugar cane stretched toward the sky. Wherever kissed by this blessing of wetness, the parched desert opened in flower.

Approaching don Celso's hometown of Salas, it seemed that nothing had changed since my last visit. Burros still lumbered down dusty roads, sagging under the weight of the fresh-cut cane stalks that they carried. Their barefoot owners still urged them toward the simple mills where the juice would be squeezed and boiled.

Cutting cane and loading burros was something I knew well from my years of apprenticeship with don Celso. In addition to serving his community as a *maestro curandero,* a master shamanic healer and teacher of the ancient wisdoms, he was a master magician and true alchemist when it came to distilling the sugar-cane squeezings into rum.

"It has to be green," he would admonish us, his machete flashing like lightning in the field. He held his glistening bronze body with light-grace as a dancer, cutting only the stalks that he sought. As his other apprentices and I would load the cut cane to be processed, he would remind us, "Remember to keep it green. The young cane that still yields to the wind is what produces the sweetest elixir."

Keep it fresh. Be open to the teachings of each moment. Let go of the need to be perfect. Model your life on the wisdoms of nature. These were the lessons of the cane-field. They were the essence of his shamanic teachings too. As I passed by the sauntering burros, I smiled as I remembered again.

Finally arriving at don Celso's modest adobe home, I stepped out of the car and gratefully stretched my aching legs. Chickens scattered in all directions as I shouted my greeting and stepped over the threshold. Standing upon the hard mud floor, we greeted one another warmly. We sat and settled in to catch up.

After a time, I brought up the reason for my visit. "*Maestro,*" I began softly, "there are rumors circulating that you are preparing to depart for the higher realms, the heavenly abode. What's this about?"

"That's right," he said simply.

"But, *maestro,* you still have a full head of hair, and your skin is still soft and smooth like that of a young man. I just can't fathom this," I insisted.

Although dressed in the tattered shirt and the well-mended ancient pants he always wore, his bearing was regal as he spoke. He sat in his favorite wooden chair, sipping a small glass of the finest, smoothest cane alcohol he had crafted. As he brought the glass to his lips, he drank slowly, honoring the labor of love that created it. The sale of this homemade rum had, over the years, fed his family. These sales freed him to spend time and energy serving his community with his shamanic vocation as well. I could feel his gratitude for that gift in every sip that he took.

"My son, remember to look beyond my physical form, use your inner sight to gaze beyond. What is it that you see now?" I closed my eyes. I looked. I gazed, just as he had taught me to do. With my inner sight, I did not see him sitting there at all. I could not feel any life force, and I knew what he had declared to be true. Honoring his pronouncement and his simple, honest life, I opened my eyes and gently took his hand. As our eyes met, I told him, "*Maestro*, I love you. You can count on me."

Then don Celso met my gaze. His voice strengthened with the urgency of his message as he spoke. "You know our people are a bunch of idiots. They use the magic of these ancestral ways unwisely. Their actions feed the engine of fear that drives the desperate. You know that if people continue to use these powers to try to achieve selfish desires and for personal gain, we are all going to be screwed."

"My son," he continued, "I need your help. We all need your help. Take what I have taught you to your adopted homeland. Take the *kamasqa*, the power of creation you have been gifted during your long apprenticeship with me to people up north. Use your perfect English and your years of training in U.S. universities to open their eyes! Because when the *gringos* see this work, they are going to wake up. They are going to want to learn these ancient wisdoms to carry creation forward and to become healers themselves. And as the *gringos* recognize and honor the ancient ways, our people here will begin to honor these too. We all need these wisdoms to endure the changes that are coming. My son, you have seen the truth of my dreaming. Trust me. Pay attention to me now and promise me this. I bequeath this lineage to you now."

As he finished speaking, I looked deep into his eyes and squeezed his hand.

"As you command, let it be so, *maestro*," I affirmed.

This was my pact and my agreement. And it is in fulfillment of this pact that I share these wisdoms with you now.

CHAPTER 1

TRUSTING SOUL/THE ART OF COMMUNING WITH OUR TRUE NATURE

*By doing one learns, through dreaming one creates, with study
one refines, in loving one fulfills—such are the wisdoms
for tending to the secret garden of our soul.*

The Challenge of Trusting Soul: How Can We Make Sense of Our Suffering?

As she moves toward the kitchen, she winces, teeth clenched against the pain. Walking has become a two-edged sword, each step taken as nerve endings scream a bitter reminder that she can still feel her feet. How long does she have until the burning is replaced by loss of feeling, loss of control, loss of mobility? The ruthless progression of her disease has robbed her of her dreams. *"Why me!"* she cries again and again. Who can possibly be served by such suffering?

Countless times each and every day, someone, somewhere, anguishes. The oldest question in the world forms on pain-contorted lips. "If there is a God, a Supreme Being of Divine Creation, *why* is there such suffering? Why is this happening to me? Why here? Why now?"

Illness and pain and death are certainly part of our human experience and impossible to avoid during our earth-walk. Yet what we must remember is the divine harmony behind even the most intractable of illusory appearances. Illness and pain can be great medicine, as strange as that may sound. Our suffering can awaken us to life's greater purpose when we remember that, while pain is inevitable, suffering is always optional. To clear the resistance is to heal. To clear the resistance is to become whole (which is the same as to heal). The pain may remain—or it may not—yet as we reclaim our inherent wholeness, suffering is transmuted and we grow strong.

As I have come to realize through my life's journey, the purpose of our human embodiment is, actually, to grow a soul. Like the making of a body during nine months of gestation, soul-making is also a process. For, although we are born with it, our soul continues to develop with every life experience. Our sufferings are simply the secretions that add to its luster—like a pearl inside an oyster. Making soul is the process of a lifetime, or several lifetimes. Mystics, saints, and shamans of ages past and of today, from places far and near, refer to this eternal sojourn in many ways, yet whatever terms are used implies a conscious engagement with our true potential as divine partners in creation. This is what it means to "grow a soul." This is what it means to commune with our essential nature.

I realize now that the best way to make sense of my personal journey from darkness to light, from the constricting childhood illness and family dysfunction which framed my suffering to the expansive awareness of all the lessons contained within it is to simply honor the Great Originating Mystery. The humility that came as I fell upon my knees in surrender when my suffering became unbearable opened me to directly experience the Divine. Like the traveler who stands on the edge of a great canyon or feels himself small while gazing at the sky, the awe inspired by the suffering that overwhelmed me provided the same release. This is why it is important to remember that traditional societies, where shamanic healing is the norm, do not define evil, harm, or ill fortune as negative. Instead, misfortune is understood as a necessary challenge for the growth and evolution of the soul. The humility that comes as we surrender to the circumstances of whatever challenges face us becomes our greatest ally for transformation.

Trust is that which provides us the means to endure the challenges, anxieties, the fears, doubts, and insecurities that are necessary for the soul's growth. Trusting soul means shifting consciousness from a place of feeling victimized by life circumstances to a place of recognizing how illness or violence or disaster are the necessary compost that creates fertile ground for Becoming. This evolution toward enlightenment requires a radical transformation of our relationship to the Creator/Creatrix as we say yes to the sacred opportunity that is our birthright. And that is the purpose of our earth-walk: to heal, to re-pattern, and to reclaim our power as we bring the world into being with our dance.

The Soul Re-members

I was born in Lima, Peru, on August 21, 1951. My coming back into wholeness as a soul on this good earth began at first breath. This divine ally of both earth and heavens filled me with so much more than oxygen in that first awakening. Spirit itself filled my lungs as life took hold. My Peruvian physician father looked lovingly upon me as I breathed. My Italian-American mother relaxed.

Yet what began so easily became a struggle for survival as I grew. As asthma set in, my breath was simply not available. I felt distant from Spirit, distant from life itself at those times. I was a young soul encased within a physical body. As a seed that has not yet sprouted, my soul lay dormant deep underground. Rather than expansion and growth, my soul contracted in order to survive. Rather than movement, it welcomed stillness. Rather than the radiant sunlight of day, it came to anticipate the darkness of an artificial harbor.

"Come out from under that table," I remember my fourth-grade teacher Mrs. Montiel telling me. In my first nine years, I had learned many ways to appear sane as my family descended ever further into dysfunction. My mother suffered from severe depression, made worse by the impulsive decision to follow my father back to his homeland after his graduate studies in the United States. Seduced by love, she left all she knew to come to a land whose language and culture she did not understand. Now her deepening depressions and repeated hospitalizations—complete with electroshock treatments to "cure" her—had taken her ever farther away from me. Each time she returned from the hospital, the arguments and tears became more pronounced. Divorce was imminent, yet my mother refused. Disagreements turned into literal battles. Plates were thrown and bones broken. I screamed in desperation the day I came upon her sitting on the bed, my father gripped between her knees as she attempted to strangle him with a belt. I watched in terrified wonder the day she chased him down the hall with a kitchen knife and knocked him to the bottom of the stairs, where he lay unconscious as she slammed an iron into his head. In the corridors of my childhood, violence and danger had become the norm. The more my mother felt betrayed, the more I felt abandoned.

In the midst of all the chaos, my breathing became more and more constricted. Sometimes I held my breath for fear I would be heard and simply add to the chaos and the stress. My asthma attacks became more frequent. I began to withdraw. I missed day after day of school as I struggled just to breathe. And even on the days I came to school, my fifth year of elementary education was lost to worry and uncertainty. Defiant. Silent. Some administrators even concluded I was cognitively impaired. Not fit for the classroom at all. "We cannot give him the help he needs here," they said. Yet in the 1960s, the type of help available was the same my mother had received during her stays at the psychiatric hospitals: Medication. Electro-convulsive therapy. Long, sterile white hallways that ended in nothing. My parents refused the advice, begging and bribing the school to keep me a while longer. Meanwhile, I found refuge in small spaces, under tables, in corners. I crawled around in the classroom as perplexed children pointed fingers, laughing and mocking me. I was like a scared animal. Hiding.

That day under the table, my father walked into the classroom. He got on his knees and extended his hand. I remember the calloused fingers when I put my hand in his. He brought me into his arms and held me tenderly as he spoke with Mrs. Montiel. I could feel his love for me then.

When we arrived home, the street was littered with his clothes, his books and papers, and all the heirlooms that normally sat on his desk in the upstairs study. All his belongings had been hurled from the second-floor windows above. My mother had had a crisis, spiraling out of her ability to tolerate the lies and contradictions that she had been promised would not be part of this, her third, marriage. She had snapped.

My father turned the door handle, but it did not budge. The locks had been changed. There was no access into the house. I panicked. For, in spite of the chaos, it was the only place where I felt safe. It was a safety that I found in illness. Even when I was bedridden, my bed was something I knew and found some comfort in. This illness was a place that had my imprint.

The most severe asthma attack that I can recall occurred at that moment. My father rushed me to a nearby clinic. Once there, I knew the routine, I knew the drill. Lie down, little Oscar, roll up your sleeve. Allow us to put this small prick into your vein, and let us run the elixir that will open up your lungs. Dexamethasone. O.5 mg, slow drip in saline solution. My breath returned. My brother Ronald, who had just been discharged from the army because of a crisis of nerves in the Korean War, came and brought me home. I understood that my father was not welcome. I went to my room. I cried, sobbing, in my loneliness and loss.

Now I understand the true miracle of love that was at the root of my illness. The asthma that was part of my life for so long had been the very path to my redemption. It pointed the way for my return to wholeness. It paved the road from the dark night of my aching soul to the superior realms of my shamanic ancestors. Even then, I felt a stirring as we rode up the winding roads away from sea-level Lima into the central Andes.

As we traveled, we followed the river Rimac, called such by Quechua-speaking peoples of the highlands because it is the river of the "one-who-speaks." My destiny was calling out to me and I could feel the murmuring voices of my ancestors tumble down the mountainsides into its flow.

It was later that same year. I was ten years old, and the finest physicians in Lima had concurred that my very survival depended on this move. As we left the coast with its smog, humidity, and pollution, the sky brightened. Irrigated fields flanked the winding road from Lima toward the Central Highlands as we drove.

Our destination was the town of Chosica, halfway between the coast and the highest peaks of the Andes, where mountain lords are named and honored with ritual offerings even now. There, high above the village, giant stones and enigmatic citadels are venerated today, just as they were during ancestral times. The entire region is known as a place of visitation, of sightings, and actual contact with star-beings. My father chose Chosica hoping that the drier, cleaner air might help my hypoxia. It was there where I found breath through an encounter with the beyond.

It was a December night in 1961. The air was cold and the sky was full of stars. My mother had put me to bed and then returned to the kitchen to clean up after dinner. From deepest slumber, I awoke with a start. My eyes were wide and round in surprise and growing desperation. My mouth was just a slit, and I felt my chest disappearing. My body was completely numb: There was no breath at all. Panic cannot even describe the sensation. I tried desperately to call for help, yet I could not move or speak. The world began closing in on me as darkness pressed down against my chest. The earth opened to swallow me, and I felt myself pulled down through the mattress of my bed, deeper and deeper into this abyss. My body felt cold. The pounding in my ears that was my heart became faint, then fainter still; then all was silent. I relaxed and fell into total drowning. I was dead.

From far away, I began hearing someone call my name. It wasn't my birth name at all, but a nickname my father had given me years before because of my curiosity and my countenance. Eager Beaver, he had called me, or Beaver for short. It felt good to have an animal name. I identified with it. Faintly, I began hearing it in my right ear, then in my left, "Beaver, Beaver, come back. We need you. Beaver, come back, Beeeeaver . . . ." Suddenly, with a gasp of air, I was pulled from the abyss that had swallowed me. I found myself sitting upright in my bed in total darkness.

With open eyes, I gazed around the room. Slowly, as I regained consciousness more fully, I began to feel the presence of extraordinary compassion. I felt indescribable love, healing, and grace. As I gazed deeper into the darkness, there appeared a quivering field of luminosity that gradually settled into three human-like forms. Standing seven feet tall, their heads were almost touching the low ceiling of my room. As they became increasingly more detailed and separate, their appearance became discernible. It was evident that they were three beings. All three had long white beards and luminous blue eyes. They were ancient, yet ageless; wizened, yet completely unencumbered. They wore long, white robes, and their long hair grew into wispy trails of luminous, spiraling light. They were three angelic beings, three Shining Ones. I now know them to be three expressions of the Divine that have been described in tales and legends since the dawn of time: luminous beings, they were strange visitors from other worlds, from unseen dimensions. They resonated and pulsed, vibrated, and shone forth. They were perfect, harmonious, whole. They were beyond all dichotomy and division. They were absolute Love.

These three beings communicated in unison a thought that mirrored exactly what I felt. A resounding gift of awakening to my true place of origin reverberated deep within me. The thought-feeling coursed from my head throughout the entire length of my body as they stood before me. It felt pleasant, like the vibrational lingering of sacred words once spoken. In that moment, my entire experience of being in a physical body shifted. I recognized my own essence in the same light that they embodied.

That awareness alone would have been enough for me to embrace the experience of death that had come upon me. In that instant, I could have just let go, returning with a peaceful heart to the hands of our Maker. Yet somehow I knew it was not my time.

No sooner did I know it than the radiant shining one to my left bent his tall frame toward me as if he were a radiant tree, a supple willow of dangling light. As he bent forward, he left traces and wisps of luminosity. As he moved, curls of spiral radiance trailed behind. He placed his transparent lips to my chest. He began to breathe the asthma out from my lungs into himself. For what seemed an eternity, he sucked in through his lips, extracting from my frail body all residue of the illness that had accompanied the evolution of my soul in this lifetime. Afterward, he raised his head and offered that density in breath up to the heavens. As he released the breath, a spiral, whirling wind opened to a door of light above him. I saw the crack between the worlds in that moment. All my suffering, my guilt and misconceptions were taken skyward as he blew. When he finished, the portal vanished as quickly as it had appeared.

Next, the Shining One to my right placed his right hand, with a luminous open-fingered palm, upon my sternum. He then placed his left palm on top of the right one. As he closed his deep blue eyes, I felt a concentrated willing: a bestowal of his essence into my heart. My entire being was lit from within as I lay motionless on the bed.

Meanwhile, the being who stood between the other two opened his eyes wide, looking straight ahead. His Buddha-like hands danced with flowing light. He touched his luminous fingertips together in various gestures.

Now I understand that what I saw was a kind of hand language. It was an Enochian language of light gifted by those who seeded our planet so many eons ago. Gestures that are universal codes for transmitting the Great Mysteries held and kept in the libraries of the etheric Shangri-las and lost monasteries of the world. I have seen these gestures many times since that night, in statues, sculptures, paintings, murals, and greatly venerated objects. These gestures appear ubiquitous in all our original peoples' cultures and in their art.

Once the hand gestures were complete, this Shining One rested his arms by his side and gazed toward me with his infinitely compassionate eyes. It was then that the communication between us began.

In that moment, my eyelids began feeling very heavy. I felt drowsy, as though I could sleep. But instead, I entered a realm between dream and waking where images floated seamlessly along. The first image I was gifted by that luminous being was of returning to Lima. I saw the great turmoil that would ensue as my father and mother separated, yet I saw myself being free of asthma forever more. I saw myself being able to run and jump and ride a bicycle as well as swimming in the ocean and playing in the schoolyard. I saw myself with my classmates, having crushes and experiencing the fullness of that very sensitive age between late childhood and young adulthood.

In that place of the in-between, words, sound, and language as we know it do not serve. Instead, communication occurs with imagery: panoramic vistas show time and space as one unified moment. In that place that is blessed by the perfection of the present, the ultimate is revealed. There, all is seen, yet little must be remembered for memory of all that the Ultimate reveals would only distress even the most advanced soul. The infinity of vision and possibility contained in the Great Mystery Teachings of these shining ones would simply be too much to bear. Yet over time, and only as needed for the soul's evolution, what is shared with the dream-traveler in that space of the Eternal Present may suddenly be made available to the memory.

The telepathic transmission of the events of my life was extensive: the jobs I would hold, the relationships I would treasure, the children who would be born and those who would be lost to me in the dance of eros that accompanies the search for self. I saw the teachers I would meet, and I saw the artistry of what I was born to do as my service to the great web of life. As the movie of my life began to fade from view, the last message reverberating through the depths of my soul was this: "Remember the rituals. Remember the rituals. Remember the rituals."

From Seed to Sprout: Soul-Making

The key to personal and planetary healing is the same: one must live in awareness of the I AM.

For the next several years, my recollection of that transformational moment was clouded. But when I met don Celso, when I began practicing the rituals of my ancestors, the memory of that moment was released in me again. It was then, when I began to quiet myself, communing with the Mystery from a place of deepest surrender to wholeness, that I came to realize this truth more fully: Illness equals action without alignment. It is estrangement from the sacred as we project the causes and consequences of our suffering onto others. It comes from looking outward rather than inward for acceptance, approval, and love.

This is not to say illness has no purpose. Quite the contrary, it can call us to question everything about our lives as we enter into conversation with powers that awaken us to our true nature. Suffering can beckon us to assume new responsibilities of being human as we become aware that we are already whole. Illness leads us to a dismembering and a complete re-graphing at the deepest levels of our being.

As we come face to face with these lessons, we experience what shamanic apprentices call "the dark night of the soul." This is a descent to the inner world of our shadow-selves, where we must choose to engage all the inferior states of our being and embrace these without judgment, fear, or denial. Then, as we release to the knowing and allow for rebirth, we come into a place of deep communion with All-That-Is. The soul reveals, the mind awakens, the spirit soars, the heart delights, the body dances. It is this shift in consciousness—from judgment to tolerance, from denial to acceptance, from separation to wholeness, and from fear to love—that is the basis for all healing that follows. Anything else is simply therapy.

So, what does this mean when applied to the suffering described above? How can illness and pain be reframed so that these are understood as more than senseless suffering? And how does the act of trusting in soul help to alleviate suffering?

The answer is simply this: In all sanctioned lineages of heartfelt shamanism the world over, the symptoms of illness are symbols of the state of your being. While you may be ill, you may be in pain, you may have experienced deep tragedy or longing, you are not just suffering passively. Instead, as you allow yourself to trust in soul and to align yourself with the process of soul-making as the reason for having a human experience to begin with, you begin to see this particular illness as a call to enter into conversation with powers that beckon you to assume new responsibilities of being human. This awareness is the beginning of healing. It is the transformation of consciousness from feeling victimized and separate to remembering that we are always connected with a higher purpose and a greater objective than simply sleep-walking. This realization liberates, moving us from feeling that we are mere victims of some random act of violence or suffering to recognizing that there is purpose in every experience of our lives. As Teilhard de Chardin once noted, we move from an understanding of being human beings having a spiritual experience to a knowing that we are spiritual beings having a human experience. And that is profoundly comforting as we journey.

Furthermore, because all healing transformation involves acknowledging that we are an interdependent part of the sacred hoop of life, as we re-member our true selves, we are inspired to act in harmony with that flow. We recognize all life as a gift. And as we receive, we participate in the flow by giving back: we give of ourselves, we give our service, we give our reverence and our gratitude. Our relationships with the earth are transformed as we enter into that awareness. We find ourselves engaging in balanced and sacred reciprocity with what is being offered and what is being received. And as we do, wholeness and sanity within the self and the world are also restored. Personal healing becomes planetary transformation.

When I entered into my pact with don Celso, when I received and agreed to carry that bequest, this is the knowledge and the practice that I agreed to shoulder. All of our planet's original peoples lived in accordance with what my ancestors called *ayni*. They practiced graceful rituals that honored the change of seasons, the cycles of the moon, the life-force energy of all the food they hunted or harvested. Sacred reciprocity is the closest English translation of this term.

This *ayni* is the essence of shamanism. As we participate, we are awakened to a power that resides *both* within us and beyond us. Shamanism is rooted in the experiential understanding that the cosmos comprises a system of correspondences. What we feel within is manifest without. What we honor above is made manifest here below. As we transform ourselves, we transform others. We are the change we wish to see in the world and, as the Hopi elders tell us, the "ones we have been waiting for."

Modern peoples, by contrast, have mainly forgotten that we live in relationship as brothers and sisters with all the beings and forces of the natural world. Our scientific redefinitions of the "unseen" as the "unreal" have caused us to forget that we are all luminous strands in a giant web of belonging. In my country, those who have tried to continue the old ways have been mainly shunned and ridiculed as ignorant, stupid people that just haven't gotten with the times.

But don Celso knew that participation in these graceful rituals has the power to restore relationship with sentient allies that do not walk on two legs. And once this right relationship is restored, we enter into dialogue with their soul-power. For, as our awakened souls are manifestations of Divinity, so are the souls of our Earth mother, the moon and sun, the sacred rainbow, the stones and trees, all plants and animals, all world teachers, our star relatives, angels, Shining Ones, and all our ancestors. And, as we reclaim our rightful place at their side as co-creators, we gain access once again to that crack between the worlds where miracles abound.

Taking don Celso's bequest seriously meant that I would walk a path of teaching graceful rituals to the "peoples of the North." It meant translating long years of apprenticeship into terms that would have resonance with my students. It resulted in the founding of what I have called the Pachakuti Mesa as a template for personal and planetary transformation. It is this foundation for transformation that I am privileged to share with you right now.

Practices for Trusting Soul: Communing with All That Is

Tuning In

In all shamanic cultures, graceful rituals help us to remember our place within the sacred hoop of life. For rituals to be the most effective, a certain process must be followed. The fundamental first step of any ritual process is to quiet ourselves and to enter into a state of common unity or "community" with all elements of the seen and unseen worlds. This act of

Communing allows us to begin to move from a state of physical awareness to a place of progressively refined vibrational frequency and sensitivity to the soul body. Shamanism is all about soul, and communing is the first step toward awakening that soul body.

So, to commune, first, find a place where you can sit quietly. Begin by breathing deeply, through the nose, with your tongue resting gently on your upper palate. Exhale all the air in your lungs and count to ten before you begin a deep, controlled breath in. Then, when you have filled your lungs to capacity, count to ten before releasing that breath, which you do as you count to ten. Repeat this a number of times while you envision your crown opening like a flower. Imagine a shaft of pure, golden light coming in through your crown and moving through your body. As you exhale, picture the soles of your feet and the palms of your hands opening to release whatever stress, tension, or density you may be feeling into the heart of *Pachamama*—Mother Earth. As Einstein reminds us, remember as you do this practice that "imagination is more important than knowledge. Knowledge is limited. Imagination encircles the world." From this state of deep communion, allow your mind to simply rest.

Bringing the past into the present moment and releasing it.

All of us have elements of our past that we are ashamed of. Coming into a place of deep acceptance of and release of all that torments us about our actions or inactions is an important aspect of being able to trust soul. An effective exercise for bringing the past into the present moment, and then releasing it into the flow of the sacred, unending circle of life, is the following. By doing this exercise during a cycle of the moon, we engage that heavenly model of ebb and flow, of filling and emptying, of going out and returning to our true selves in a way that harnesses the power of all cycles into our lives.

For this exercise, at the time of the new moon, you should first enter into a state of deep communion as described above. From this place of ease and centered awareness, allow your mind to fill with an image of a past transgression that you would like to release. Take a pen or pencil and paper and simply write some words or draw a picture of the event or behavior in which you participated that is troubling you now. After putting these words or sketches onto paper, light a small fire using kindling or a charcoal briquette in a censor or other fireproof receptacle. Give offerings of incense, sweet grass, sage, cedar, tobacco, or other ingredients that are sacred to you to the fire, knowing that the flame and smoke produced by the burning of the paper that you have prepared will be carried heavenward and gratefully received by the unseen realms.

When you feel that your intentions of loving release have been adequately prepared, simply voice a prayer of gratitude and release as you offer the paper into the flame. Wait until it has been completely consumed. After the ashes that remain have cooled, take these and mix them with equal parts of baking soda and water in a small container. Put this in the freezer until the next full moon. At that time, carry the offering to a stream or other body of running water and gently shake the ashes and baking soda mixture until these are released into the stream. As you do, know that your offering is received and that you are completely absolved of the burden that you have carried. Above all, release all attachment to the outcome, and *trust*. This is good practice for "letting go" and trusting soul.

CHAPTER 2

HONORING SPIRIT / THE ART OF CONSECRATING OUR LIVES AS LOVE

When we surrender the need to figure it all out and cultivate the ability to let it all in, then our earth walk becomes a sacred dance of healing service on the planet. More than the world needing saving, it needs loving.

The Challenge of Honoring Spirit: How Can We Know Oneness? How Can We Cultivate a Relationship with That Knowing?

Angry Muslims burn American flags as a blasphemous YouTube video circulates. An American ambassador dies. Halfway around the world, a Florida pastor declares Islam and its teachings "of the Devil" while an effigy of Muhammad hangs limp. What makes religion spawn such hatred? When will the fanaticism end?

The realm of spirit has no dogma. Its only doctrine is an invitation to become conscious of our essential nature. We are *at one* with the Great Originating Mystery which is within *and* beyond us. It is our re-membering this experience of union that returns us to wholeness. When we acknowledge the perfection within us even as we consecrate ourselves to that which is beyond, we are well aligned. Our willingness to embrace this paradox of free will and surrender is how we honor spirit in our lives.

But, if spirit is an awareness of wholeness, and a birthright to which we all have equal access, why do messages of judgment, or disdain, or intolerance seem to pervade the very air that we breathe? Western religions tell us our salvation comes as we fill ourselves up with what we lack. But they also teach that there is only *one* God, only *one* way, only *one* truth. Eastern religions take a different approach. We are already too full, these tell us. The trick is to empty ourselves out, give up who we are, surrender. In both cases, we are somehow deficient. In the midst of these messages, is it any wonder we lose sight of our transcendent or divine nature?

After years of apprenticeship with my beloved teachers of both physical and non-physical realms, I live with this heartfelt conviction: The earth-honoring traditions of our planet's original peoples provide a welcome alternative to all dogma. These traditions show us the way back to our spiritual roots as they offer us an intimate, reverent relationship with *Pachamama*, who is our beloved Earth mother. As we marvel at the patterns and the beauty of the natural world, we learn to walk in gratitude for the gift of our lives. And as we pay close attention to how her cycles, pulses, and rhythms are mirrored in ourselves, we gain a very clear understanding that we are not separate. Through this practice, we recognize ourselves as luminous strands in the great web of life.

A Time of Apprenticeship

It was the first Tuesday of August in 1969. My surf buddies had departed and the ritual had begun. The chill of evening settled around me as I gazed at the marvels of don Celso's mesa from where I sat to his right. I recognized the styles of some of the medicine pieces on his altar. As I stared in wonder, I was transfixed by their power. There on his mesa were 3,000-year-old Chavín effigies and a 1,000-year-old Chimu bowl that was filled with a mixture of fragrant tobacco and the finest cane liquor. I feel the medicine of my ancestors and my heart fills with reverence as I relive the moment of that first encounter. Herb-filled bottles called *seguros,* conch shells and rattles, Inkan mace heads, a small crucifix, and stones smooth as satin grabbed my attention. At the top of the white ground cloth that held all these pieces stood swords and knives as well as staffs of *chonta* palm and *palo santo.*

The families who had come to support their loved ones on this night huddled together in the darkness on the dirt-packed floor of the patio where the altar was set up. Wrapped in ponchos, they waited patiently as don Celso rattled and sang to all the objects on his altar; naming and welcoming all his spirit allies, he called on the living essence of their power to accompany him that night. We communed together, ritually imbibing the sacred plant medicine in gratitude for the lessons and the messages that would be shared.

Sometime later, after the tobacco offering was given and after his patients were cleansed with the sacred objects on his altar, out of the center of his *banco* a light started to circulate. I blinked my eyes in amazement. The light continued to rise from the mesa. As it emerged, it coalesced into a large, oval, pulsing field. As I continued to watch, the same three wizened Shining Ones that visited me and healed me of asthma eight years before appeared before us now. As they began to come closer, I stared in open-mouthed wonder. No one else seemed to see them, not even don Celso's assistants who were sitting just to his left. Was I dreaming? Was this really happening?

At first I didn't notice don Celso's sideways glance. Then, he elbowed me firmly, jarring me from my reverie. "Do you remember them?" he asked me. "Yes, I do," I stuttered. At that moment, my entire reality shifted. I felt transported back in time to a moment I had all but forgotten. In less than a nanosecond everything that had been shown to me at age ten during that near-death experience came back into my awareness. And I remembered it all. In this second visitation by the three Shining Ones, I tapped into the noosphere—the ineffable yet universal field of information that some call the Akashic record.

In that moment, all contrasts, all polarities, all separation, all interpretation, all need to have a nice comforting orderly world was annihilated. It was all destroyed. And I found myself floating up in space and dissolving as a separate entity, as an individual, as an ego-mind, as a personality. In that moment, the one known to this world by the name Oscar just disappeared. I was *absorbed* within the *ALL*. I remembered my purpose for being born, and this time, it stayed firmly imprinted in my psyche. All that I had witnessed and forgotten at age ten came cascading back, free of censorship and dimensional filters. I realized how incomplete our sensory experiences are as I peeked behind the veil of the eternal *now*. As soon as the ritual ended, I asked don Celso if I might apprentice with him, and he agreed.

Over the next twelve years, I spent every summer vacation returning to apprentice with don Celso. As he taught me the ways of my ancestors, I would tune in again to that field of awareness, and I would simply remember how to perform the rituals that he shared. Yet that ability to access the Akashic record—the stored essence of all life on this good earth—did not prevent me from making foolish mistakes. For it is difficult to remain awake to our true nature, even after we have glimpsed it. The ego fights mightily against our enlightenment. That is why spiritual practice is so important. It is through the rituals—through the sacrifice of our time and our energy—that we cultivate gratitude for our earth-walk. It is through the practice of offering our heartfelt thanks with cornmeal or tobacco, incense or coca leaves—whatever is sacred food for the ancestors and the spirit allies who walk with us—that we humbly remember our place in the universe. With these practices we affirm that just because we are a divine manifestation of the Great Spirit, we are in no way different or more "special" in beauty than is a blade of grass or a spiral galaxy. The rituals we practice become expressions of sacred reciprocity. Their repetition become the furrows that channel the flow of spirit so that the seeds of our compassion and right action toward others may grow strong.

At first, don Celso taught me about the sacred objects on his mesa. He taught me where they came from and how they were used. He taught me about the powers of the natural world that they harness and embody. Then he taught me how to assemble all the elements of his mesa for the evening rituals. Rather than simply memorizing the placement of all the medicine pieces or imitating his actions, he insisted I deeply commune with each piece, each *arte,* as a conscious being and trusted medicine ally that is imbued with the power of creation in every moment. Don Celso taught me, through his example, to honor the perennial vitality of each ceremonial artifact by lovingly remembering each experience of healing I had witnessed him perform with it. By evoking in every detail the image of the entity whose power it carried, I began to be able to enter into deeper and deeper communion with these shamanic spirit helpers.

As my initiations and my apprenticeship progressed, my *vista* expanded. *Vista* is a kind of shamanic clairvoyance. It is a spiritual vision that allows us to look deeply into both the unadulterated soul essence and the very human agenda of any person. *Vista* also allows one to see the person's *sombra,* or "spiritual double." This *sombra* reflects a person's psychological as well as physical traits. Further into my apprenticeship with don Celso, I learned to see a person's *sombra* coming into the healing lodge before the actual physical person arrived. I could envision if they had a limp or a particular physical deformity. I also learned to see into their psyches; their greatest fears and insecurities as well as the most elevated expression of human dignity became more available to my gaze.

After my *vista* improved, I was able to use it to diagnose the cause of a patient's illness—whether physical, emotional, spiritual, or mental. By really focusing on the *sombra,* I could see all these arenas of dis-ease. And once the diagnosis was complete, the healing-work could begin.

As don Celso taught me, healing requires two skill sets, which I was developing through my apprenticeship. First, I needed to learn how to develop and to discipline my "imagination." In the healing arts, imagination is about constructing images through the power of the mind. With loving intention, one visualizes the patient as healthy and whole. "Our task as maestros," don Celso repeatedly told me, "is to help others remember their wholeness—that they are complete just as they are." Second, I needed to learn to work in harmony with all the powers embodied on the medicine ground to raise the vibration so that the image I was holding could take form and actually manifest itself. This combination of loving intention and increased vibration is what allows "magic" to happen. It is also what allows healing transformation to occur.

This lesson became very clear to me during one particularly arduous pilgrimage with don Celso, his son, and his son-in-law. The occasion of our expedition was the impending arrival of a group from Lima for a series of healings that would require a significant amount of the sacred San Pedro cactus to be harvested and prepared. This sacred plant ally is sometimes grown in people's gardens, but the most powerful and alive of these plant relatives—and those which don Celso required for this particular healing—could only be found in a hidden corner of the Chongoyape Valley. This sacred site was about a day's walk from his home in Salas. To be effective at all, the plant needed to be harvested in an honoring way, right after it flowers, which happens only in the light of the full moon.

Unfortunately for us, this hallowed ground where the San Pedro grew happened to be accessible only by crossing into a military base. As Peru was still governed by a military dictator who had imposed martial law and a mandatory curfew, it meant that trespassers could be shot on sight. So we chose to travel stealthily, under cover of night, to avoid detection. It was the darkest time of the month, with no moon in the sky at all. My teacher had chosen this time deliberately so that the dark would hide our advance.

Before our start and all through our journey, don Celso made offerings of cornmeal and tobacco to the *apus*—the mountain guardians of this region. He invoked all his plant and animal relatives, all ancestral allies of the ancient cultures who brought forth this lineage, asking for help to complete this sacred mission so that no harm would befall us. He offered our pilgrimage in service to healing and in the name of the Great Mystery. As he did, he trusted that all would be well.

To avoid detection, we took a very roundabout way to our destination. It was an *El Niño year.* Torrential rains and mudslides had fouled the streams we had expected to drink from, and the edible plants that would normally have supplemented our rations were absent. These had been washed away or buried in the flood. The little bit of food and water that we had packed was quickly depleted. Where carob trees and bushes with edible berries had once stood, there was only mud and parched brown earth on our path. All the usual landmarks pointing our way were gone. One day's journey quickly became three as we trudged on through the barren landscape. Yet don Celso remained confident that the San Pedro cacti that we sought were still standing. His *vista* kept presenting him with a vision of the San Pedritos with their white blossoms waving at him, calling to him.

It was the driest, most inhospitable trek you can imagine. Yet after three days and nights, we finally came upon these plant allies standing alone in this eerie, moonless, landscape. Seven-ribbed San Pedros with the most beautiful, white blossoms were there, growing on a ledge with a little rock outcropping just as don Celso had envisioned. We were exhilarated to see them, yet completely exhausted, hungry, and thirsty. As we approached these beautiful medicine plants, don Celso suddenly told us to sit.

What happened next defies all description. Don Celso told us to quiet our minds, deepen our breathing, and become invisible. He had seen with his *vista* that the military police were looking for us and that they were nearby. So we steeled ourselves and we quieted ourselves. We took slow, deep breaths and we went within. We trusted in don Celso's guidance. We had no other choice if we wanted to survive.

At that moment, we began hearing the rumbling of jeep motors in the distance. We began hearing the barking of dogs. Don Celso told us that no matter what happened, we were not to open our eyes, for that would break the spell that we were weaving. He told us to be alive, yet not to be present. He insisted that any disturbance of our alignment, any breach of the shared purpose and the field of unified consciousness that we were creating would reveal where we were. The noises came closer.

The four of us sat motionless with closed eyes. The dogs and the army officials were upon us. The floodlights that were shining on us were so bright that I could see the luminosity through my closed eyelids. I could hear the panting and feel the warm breath of one of the dogs at my left ear. The soldiers were speaking to one another, "They must be around here." They were walking right next to us, dogs sniffing, literally gazing into the ground where we sat. After four or five minutes they said, "There's nobody here. Let's go check somewhere else." They got into their jeeps and drove away.

We remained motionless for a long time after they left. We were stunned by the unbelievable experience we had just passed through, afraid to utter one sound until we heard our teacher speak. When he did, he said simply, "Brothers, the light is ours. Stand up now; it's time to celebrate the protection that our beloved San Pedros have bestowed upon us."

At that moment I knew that the beautiful plant relatives that had withstood the mudslides had been waiting to offer their flesh in healing service to us. They were even flowering at the time of the new moon, which is unheard of. In this way, they were also indicating their readiness to be harvested.

Because we were impeccable in our values and our integrity, the sacred plant relatives were waiting. They had protected us from harm and were offering themselves to us because don Celso was adhering to the path of the healer in an honoring way. With offerings of gratitude and deep trust in the power of these sacred plant allies, don Celso had shown these, our San Pedro brothers, the respect that is owed them. It is a deference that has all but been forgotten. He was honoring the traditional ways. Our sacrifice, our conviction and trust in their power, our willingness to even risk our lives in healing service to others had been noted. Thus, positive outcome was assured.

What I learned through this experience was this: Loving intention, focus, and alignment with the forces and powers of nature actually molds the material world. Yet an even deeper understanding of these things was revealed as we began our trip back to don Celso's home in Salas.

After harvesting the precious medicine plants, we began our return journey. We were obviously hungry and thirsty. It had been more than three days since our rations had been consumed. At one point in the journey, don Celso asked us again to sit. He said, "You all must be very hungry. Let's see what we can do about that." And so he closed his eyes, bowed his head, put his hands in a prayerful position, and he quieted himself. As we sat there facing him respectfully opening and aligning ourselves to whatever he was doing, he put his right hand out with the palm facing upward.

There, maybe three or four inches above his right hand, a perfectly formed orange appeared out of thin air! It just dropped into the palm of his hand! From there, he let the orange fall to the earth. After this first one, a second, third, and fourth orange materialized. They were big and bright in color, just like those eating oranges that are grown in citrus valleys on the southern coast of Peru. As they appeared, they just looked like little traces of light. But as don Celso allowed them to fall to the ground, they became solid. "Serve your-selves, boys," he told us simply. So, we each picked up an orange and opened it. They were beyond succulent and juicy. They were heavenly oranges, with flesh so sweet it is hard to describe, yet the orange taste in them was beyond any orange flavor that I had tasted in my physical life until then.

I know from this experience that the veil between seen and unseen worlds is practically non-existent when one learns to walk between the worlds. I also learned that one's purity of motive and clarity of intention, especially regarding a selfless desire to help lift suffering in the world, allows for the mate-rialization of a properly sustained image or thought form. I carry this conviction because I have lived it!

What I have realized as I reflect back on these moments is that what I was seeing, tasting, and experiencing was not hap-pening on planet Earth at all. Instead, it was happening in the Superior Realm—which Andean people call the *hanaq pacha*. This is the space we call cosmic, the place we call heaven and the dimension of pure *consciousness* which flows into us from every direction. In the moment we received those succulent oranges, we returned to the Garden of Oneness—to that place where the invisible light of consciousness pours forth. This is the realm of Gaia, which is the foundation for all physical expressions on earth.

Our consecration to the Great Originating Mystery on this journey allowed us entry into a pristine experience of sacred reciprocity with the sacred web of life. And as we entered there, we experienced the glory of all the suns and stars inside one small microscopic cell of the human brain. This sacred mirroring of self-reflexive consciousness—this awareness that what is within and beyond us are the same—provided us with the ability to transform our physical world.

This consciousness, from which we absorb our very essence, is vibration. In fact, all relationship between spirit and matter, between formlessness and form, between the above and the below, is simply a matter of vibration. When we enter into that more refined vibratory frequency, we say that "magic happens." We say this because what we perceive appears impossible to our sensory conditioned, rational mind. It appears to defy all laws of Newtonian physics. But as we awaken to our oneness and attune to more refined harmonic vibrations, we realize this: Consciousness begets matter through actions that are expressed in word or gesture. Thus, access to magic is only limited by our focus, by the sacred *relationships* we cultivate through our offerings, and by the loving intention with which we walk.

Creating a loving relationship with these powers and forces was foundational for our ancestral peoples. It was understood at the first great seeding of our world. Our ritual practices today are a stepping-stone toward mastery of these once widely practiced arts. This is what shamanic apprenticeship is all about! And when these rituals are practiced

together with others, we are able to generate a field of unified consciousness that is capable of raising the vibrational
frequency all the more easily. When we become the light of
consciousness in *community*, our true nature and our power
are revealed: We re-member who we really are and who we are
destined to be.

As I continued my apprenticeship with don Celso, he
taught me how to divine the dynamics behind an illness, to
call lost vitality back to the suffering with rattle and song, and
to cleanse with the medicine pieces from his mesa the psycho-
emotional density produced by fearful living that patients
carried. He initiated as well as apprenticed me to his teaching.

In one kind of initiation, he taught me to identify and
to harvest the plant medicines that could cure his patients of
"God-given" ailments like arthritis or respiratory infections.
His pharmacy was the natural world, where remedies grew
wild on the desert floor or in the deep shadow of the nearby
mountains. I remember these times of the new moon when
don Celso would rouse his other assistants and me very early
in the morning. "Let's go and take a little walk, boys," he
would say. And we'd start off at dawn on a walk that would
seem endless, with little or no water. We would hike for hours
toward the mountains, through scrub brush and thorns in
order to find these precious remedies. At noon, under the
sweltering sun, he would say, "We're almost there, it's just
right over that next little hill." After several more hours of
interminable walking, we would get to a place that was right
at the foothills of the Chongoyape mountains. Then he would
call one of us over, and he'd say, "Okay, so when a little purple
flower comes up on this plant, it will be ready to harvest. So
the next full moon, you come back and you harvest this if

it has a little purple flower." And then we would have to go back home empty-handed, only to return again two weeks later. For that one teaching, we'd walk all day, arriving back at his home exhausted at dusk. This was the nature of my apprenticeship; it was about practice and respect, it was about patience and an embodied kind of knowing that comes only from experience and time.

Another kind of initiation required me to come face to face with my deepest fears while learning to embrace all the raw powers of an enchanted world. After I had fasted and refrained from all forms of sensual pleasure in order to purify myself, don Celso would send me out in the middle of the night to wait on a vision at ancient ruins, where the shades of my ancestors still roam. I would spend the night there, armed with my trust in the powers of his mesa, the animal allies, and the unlimited love, the eternal compassion and the field of protection that he had taught me. There, by myself under the stars, surrounded by scorpions and snakes, pumas, and tarantulas as well as by the mythical powers of the unseen realms, I would have to conquer my fears, slow my galloping heart, offer my aromatic waters, my flower petals and tobacco to establish bonds of sacred reciprocity with that holy place. Then, as my ancestors had done before me, I would spend the night there, entering into a space of quiet, grateful prayer, where I would trust and wait. What would come was both tangible and intangible, both a revelation of alliance and another gift to be incorporated into the altar. Sometimes it was a stone relative. But it might also be a staff or potsherd from the Chimu or Lambayeque ancestors who still inhabit these ancient graveyards.

These rigorous rites of passage did much more than provide me with plant and animal shamanic allies to assist in my healing. These disciplined encounters with my deepest anxieties opened me to the crucial importance of an intimately transformative relationship with myself. As I became more and more sensitive through these initiations, I entered into a world that was more of dreaming than of thinking, more of an imagining than of a structuring, and more a journey than a destination. As I opened myself more deeply to the Cloud of Unknowing, as I released expectations and concrete definitions of what "must be" for a willingness to ally myself with the formless, I began to have access to more elevated expressions of the power within creation. I began to be aware that I could choose which form would best serve the recipient of my prayers and my medicine, commanding it, decreeing it, calling it forward into service.

Don Celso was infinitely patient with me at every step of my apprenticeship. Some days I would just need to get away and ride the waves that were pumping down in Huanchaco, which was only a couple of hours away from his house. I would feel that my own *sombra* was already in Huanchaco, and it was everything I could do to stay with him. "Don Celso," I would say, "I need to go to the beach. I can't sleep here tonight." "Yeah, okay, son, go on ahead," he would respond. "Just be careful."

After a few days kicking back in a hammock on some old surf bum's front porch, I would show up again to don Celso's adobe house wearing the arrogance of my youth as proudly as my surf-gear. Then, he would simply stare at me with his piercing eyes and say, "What's going on with you, Oscar? Your river doesn't seem to be running too deep today. Have you been smoking that Devil weed again?" Because that was one thing he wouldn't tolerate. He did not want me ever to show up to do any work with him if I had been using any mind-altering substance in a recreational manner. He knew that it was part of the times to be experimenting with psycho-tropic substances in one way or another, especially for us surfing types. He expected that. Yet I understood that it was fiercely forbidden for me to bring that vibration into his lodge, or even into his home.

So, on those days when I returned from Huanchaco, I would cringe. I hoped he wouldn't look into my eyes and see the shallowness of my river. In those times, I also felt how the flow of spirit into my body was being hindered by my ego, my lack of respect for the sacred nature of life, my lust, or just my unconscious stupor. I still made stupid mistakes. Even though I had started to pay more attention to what I had been shown at age ten and reminded of when the Shining Ones appeared to me again out of the center of his altar, I still lapsed into impulsive, unconscious living. I was still young and I needed much ritual practice to remain consciously connected to spirit and to the divinity residing within me.

Further Lessons of My Apprenticeship

Honoring spirit is about becoming aware that you are one with the Great Mystery in a liquid, fluid universe. It is about being willing to enter the ocean of possibility, trusting that a Source greater than yourself is guiding your journey. This isn't the same as abandoning the "gift" of free will. In fact, the presence of your ability to choose, in every moment, whether or not to follow these "nudges" is at the heart of honoring spirit.

As individual souls, we all ultimately must embark upon a sojourn of merging embrace with our Creator. This may take lifetimes or it may come quickly, depending on how open we are to the lessons of our earthly incarnation. That is what our soul's progression and what spiritual maturation is all about.

What all famed mystics and spiritual leaders of our earth's original peoples knew is this: We are all children of the earth and sky who carry the divinity of creation within. The prayers that we offer, our words of invocation to the Great Originating Mystery, the sacred languages of correspondence between that which is within and without—these are powers well known to the hermetic adepts and to the spiritual leaders of our planet's most ancient civilizations. Furthermore, what we *think,* what we *say,* and what we *do* matters, for we co-create, sanctify, and renew the world "as above, so below," with our intention. Our language begets our reality. And as we reclaim the power of language in this way, we contribute to a flourishing of divine harmony that is sustainable. The focus is on this rather than on the "saving" of our isolated souls.

Before spirituality became religion, before *at-One-ment* became atonement, before the power that every human holds as co-creator became subverted by religious politics and power, we understood how we are connected in ways we have long since forgotten. We understood our relatedness with all living things and we knew the responsibility that this related-ness brings with it. We have mainly forgotten this message. It is time to remember it now.

Religion is an easy target to scapegoat for this amnesia, but it is not religion alone that is to blame for our forget-ting. Religion has provided a useful tool for the cultivation of wisdom, compassion, and right action toward others.

Jiddu Krishnamurti spoke of the church as a flowerpot in his teachings. As the vehicle that connects what is most important in our lives with the same mythologies and cosmologies that guide others, religions are useful. Religions hold the soil that nurtures the seeds of spirituality and connection that we plant. They create the conditions that allow these seeds to grow and bear fruit.

Yet the great Krishnamurti also told that when the sapling becomes too large for the flowerpot, you have to break the mold and transplant the sapling into the deep, rich soil of our beloved Earth mother in order to save it. Only in that larger space of collective experience—in that larger space of universal wisdom and cosmic information that is the Akasha—will the sapling grow to maturity. Only then can its lofty canopy and mature root system bridge the worlds and breathe spiritual life back into the world.

Thus, while all religions have their purpose because they can provide a framework for understanding our experiences, we must never bow mindlessly to the authority of any human emissary. Instead, honoring spirit is accomplished as we quiet ourselves, eliminating the chatter of our doubting minds so that we can hear our heart pulsing with gratitude for the sacred gift that is life. As we do this, we awaken to the invisible light of consciousness that flows from the heavens to fill us. Like a flower responding to the sun's life-giving rays, we open to love.

Each of us has catalyzing moments that open us to an awareness of Source within ourselves. Like many who recognize the power of the spiritual in their lives, it was the depth of my suffering that primed the pump of my awakening. As I opened to my reality of being born "of spirit" as much as "of matter," I gained an expanded view of myself. I allowed Love to be Who-I-Am. In this awakening, I connected more deeply with myself. And in so doing, I entered into a true sacred alliance of healing service with All My Relations.

Don Celso taught me these things through example. He kept me green, kept me a learner, kept me from feeling that I had "mastered" the lessons, which only slows the flow of spirit and the revelation of soul in our lives. At first my own ego resisted these lessons. In the early years of my apprenticeship, I was still subject to the whims of my ego, to lower emotions and impulsive acts that I engaged in without much reflection. Rather than being the master of my free will, I was subordinate to my desires. My feelings were dominated by others as I reacted to each affront that I perceived. I was victim to, rather than master of, the dysfunctional environment in which I lived. It took me a long time to give up my insistence on the illusion of being "in charge." For years, I struggled mightily against myself. But as I finally found peace through my surrender to spirit, I began living the wisdom that transcends all understanding. Then I began to penetrate the hidden dimensions of life. And I began to be able to truly serve others.

The challenges that don Celso put before me took me to the very edge of madness. The courage to continue my apprenticeship came as a consequence of my willingness to continue with the practices he gave me. This definition of faith—not as blind acceptance but as conviction and as a tool for carrying on—became my greatest ally. This grew as I continued to be willing to just show up to do the work. And the rituals and simplicity of lifestyle that I practiced helped me realize that the entire world was my ally.

Along the way, it became obvious that I needed to cultivate and to practice earth-honoring ceremonies in order to continue to walk in beauty. This is how I came to develop the Pachakuti Mesa Tradition which is a ritual *practice* that integrates the ceremonial arts of the Shining Ones and those of our beloved *Pachamama's* ancestral shamanic cultures. These practices restore sacred trust between humankind and the natural world. They create a proven template for honoring spirit that works—that is, if *you* work it.

Practices for Honoring Spirit: Consecrating Our Lives as Love

Honoring the Divinity within Ourselves: Toning the I-AM

"In the Beginning was the Word...and the word was God," the Bible tells us. Before the beginning, the Brahman (absolute reality) thought, "I am only one—may I become many." This caused a vibration that became sound, which set creation itself into motion.

Thus, wise spiritual leaders—in both Eastern and Western traditions—knew that vibration is creation. By extension, uttering certain frequencies can restore wholeness to a fractured being, no matter the species. So often in our daily lives, we attend to the needs of the body or of the mind, but we forget that the spirit also requires nurturing to bring ourselves into balance. And it is when body, mind, and spirit are all in balance that we come into more intimate contact with ourselves, re-membering ourselves as whole. To come into an awareness of at-One-ment, I recommend the following practice.

Sit in a chair that fully supports your body and that allows your back to be comfortably straight. Rest your feet on the floor slightly apart with your heels together, and put your hands in your lap with your right hand in your left palm and your thumbs gently touching. If you have ever noticed Egyptian depictions of the ancient pharaohs, you will see this same position depicted. It is a position that helps to anchor the energy we are working within our bodies in a very helpful way.

Begin by taking three deep breaths, through the nose, with your tongue gently resting on the upper palate of your mouth. You should consciously fill your belly first and then let the breath move up into your lungs, filling your lungs to capacity and holding to the slow count of ten. Remember, as you breathe in oxygen, you are breathing in life force, or *prana*. As you breathe, open your crown chakra and feel the clear light of consciousness that descends from the heavens. Feel this breath enter and fill you. As you continue to breathe, you are literally bringing spirit into your physical being. This deep breathing is, thus, in-spiration.

On your next inhalation, you begin toning I-AM. As you do so, remember that this toning is an offering as well as an awakening, for there is sacred reciprocity in all things. Start on any note of the scale that is comfortably low by toning aaaaaahhhhhh. This is the vowel sound that creates the vibration that opens the heart chakra. As you continue to vocalize, slide your voice up a full octave and let the aaaaahhhh become eeeeeeeeee. Thus, you have the "I" which sounds like "aaaaaahhhh-eeeeeee." The eeeeee sound creates the vibration that is perfectly suited to aligning with the higher realms. As you tone this sound, it gives the same vibration as that of bells, chimes, and Tibetan *tingshas*. When you have offered all your breath to this two-pitched aaahh-eee, pause and breathe. Then return to the first pitch—which is a full octave lower than the "eeee" ending of the two-pitched "I" sound you have just completed. Breathe in and tone "AM," drawing out the vowel and the consonant so that it sounds like "aaaaammm." This vocalization draws spirit into the belly, crystalizing it firmly in the physical plane.

Repeat this process, toning "I-AM" as you draw out each vowel and also the "m" sound, seven times to complete the practice. As you complete this process, at least once per day for seven days and then at least once per week for seven weeks, you may begin to feel a significant shift in your perception. Your head may tingle. You may feel lighter. You may become much more aware of how balanced you feel. But even if you don't, do not worry. Just trust the process and do the practice. Keep showing up for yourself, without attachment to outcomes. Keep your vision focused on that positive expression of the I-AM principle that you are speaking.

This I-AM is the spirit that is within you and beyond you. If you keep your vision focused on the positive expression of your own divinity as you do this toning, you will invariably *become* that awareness. I guarantee it. You just have to keep showing up for the work. All you need is trust. Nothing else is required.

Consecrating the Ground of Your Beauty Walk

By performing ritual "feedings" and consecrated offerings to the natural world you are able to harness and commune with the spiritual forces within creation. You access multiple dimensions of being and begin to understand your own immortal self through a direct experience of the sacred in

life. By engaging in sacred reciprocity with the raw forces of
nature as well as the spiritual powers present in the area where
you make your offerings, you deepen your awareness of interdependence with all life's dimensions. And your relationship
with all that is sacred opens you to your divine birthright as
co-creator, as transformer, as healer. This is the purpose of the
earth-honoring rituals embodied in the Pachakuti Mesa.

To begin to create your own mesa, with medicine pieces
that are (ideally) gifted to you from the natural world, make a
practice of walking in nature and making offerings to the trees
that you pass, the streams that you cross, and the landscapes
that you encounter. Make offerings to the warmth of the sun
in the morning, the guiding light of the moon after nightfall,
to the cold wind that carries energy from the heavens, and to
the earth beneath your feet that holds you firmly grounded
on this plane. As you walk along, know that your entire life
is a pilgrimage and that each footfall is sacred. While it is
certainly enough to be thankful as you journey, it is helpful
to carry physical offerings with you in a small medicine bag
as you walk. These can be tactile reminders as well as "prayer-
holders" that help you focus your energies and love. These
can help bring your awareness again to the *ayni*—the sacred
reciprocity of give-and-take—that is an inherent part of your
sacred journey.

In the shamanic cultures of our planet's original peoples, the most valuable food and medicine gifts of the natural world were those that were offered back to the earth in
thanksgiving. Thus, Native peoples of North America—or
Turtle Island—carry and offer tobacco. In Central America—
Serpent Island—it is corn pollen and cornmeal that are the
equivalent. In South America—Heart Island—coca *kintus*

are the most sacred of offerings. *Kintus* are three perfect coca leaves arranged like a *fleur de lis* between the second and third fingers of one's hand and prayed over before being given. Flowers, songs, prayers, seeds, grains, colored sand, cloth, clay effigies, incense, candles, oil, food and wine, blood, and even the act of walking or dancing are just a few among many other examples of offerings that are given in gratitude for the gifts we receive from the Mother. Yet what you carry in your offering bag is less important than the prayers of gratitude and honoring that enliven these gifts as you give them.

For this practice, take time to give offerings every time you walk in nature. Cultivate an awareness of gratitude as you gently blow prayers into your most sacred offerings—whether cornmeal or tobacco or oil or flowers or whatever these may be. Then sprinkle these prayers, carried by the material offerings in which they are now embodied, where you stand. In this way, you release your loving intention into the landscape. Now stop and *observe* the beauty. Notice the intricate patterns and the wisdom of nature with every plant and animal perfectly adapted to its niche. Breathe in the interdependence and relatedness of all process. Allow yourself to open up to the awe.

As you engage in this practice, know that your gifts are received and begin to be open to return gifts in kind. See in the stone that calls to you the gift of foundation; an irrefutable connection to the earth. Hear the sound of the waves and the flow of life's cycles in the shell that washes up on the shore. Recognize the feather of the bird that lies before you as the message: Your prayers have been carried skyward! Be attentive and you will begin to be transformed. The earth is your teacher and there is so much to learn!

As you begin working with the elements that you collect on your pilgrimage, your own Pachakuti Mesa will begin to emerge. As you begin assembling these pieces in a specific order, an experience of interpersonal wholeness and transpersonal harmony with Mother Earth will be fostered. Pick up these gifts, whatever gifts call to you, with gratitude as you leave a token of your deepening awareness of relationship in return. Open yourself to the lessons and the signs. These are the origins of the healer's mesa, and each sacred medicine piece has a story and a message. As they reveal themselves to you, sit in quiet meditation and listen. Let spirit speak through these as you open yourself to their guidance. This is how you consecrate your beauty-walk and honor spirit in your life.

CHAPTER 3

OPENING HEART/THE ART OF COMPOSING LIFE AS SACRED RELATIONSHIP

Teach love by the way you live . . .

The Challenge of Opening Heart: How Can We Embody Love in the Midst of Our Woundedness?

"Why doesn't he love me anymore?" She lies alone on the bed, doubled-up in despair. Her heart is aching with a hollowness that echoes in her chest. She cries aloud to the emptiness, "Where did I fail him? It is my fault that he has gone! I don't deserve to be loved!" The tears flow, but they do not cleanse. Instead they mirror the self-loathing and the blame she heaps upon herself. Will she ever learn to forgive herself enough to allow love into her life again?

The wounds of loneliness and disenchantment lead to such despair. As I see it, learning to cultivate sacred relationship is *the* most important skill we need to develop in order to heal. Learning to give and to receive, to forgive, to accept and to *honor* ourselves as well as others—these are the aptitudes and the attitudes that will redeem us. "You do unto yourself as you do unto others." Sacred relationship is as simple as that.

The awareness of our basic interdependence is what will bring the change we seek. When we finally grow new eyes and ears with which to see and hear the ancient wisdom stories of relationship—stories that are modeled on the profound interdependence that lies everywhere before us in the natural world—we will begin to finally understand. Then we will walk gently, with reverence, as we remember our sacred partnership with the earth.

Because the self and the Circle of Life are mere reflections of a single whole, our relations with our inner demons, with one another, and with our Mother Earth can be no different. Thus, we must become willing to nurture ourselves, befriending both the shadow and the light in every aspect of our lives. As we do, we cultivate and celebrate an "attitude of gratitude" that is projected outward. As we learn to love ourselves, the pristine reflection that we carry in our hearts becomes a healing salve for the world.

When we wake up to realize that we are not separate—that all duality is illusion—teaching love by the way we live becomes much easier. The shamanic life is all about this reverence. It is about opening our hearts to honoring all the gifts we receive as we walk upon the earth—gifts of beauty and of nourishment, of wisdom and of our very lives.

A New Apprenticeship

Bleary-eyed, I stared again at the piles of scholarship applications that lay before me on the rickety wooden table. The single hanging bulb that illuminated my windowless workspace flickered annoyingly. This wasn't at all what I imagined when Dr. Fernando Cabieses approached me in 1982 as I ended my two-year post-graduate fellowship in ethnopsychology at Emory University that had been sponsored by the Organization of American States. At that time, Cabieses had introduced me to don Benito Corihuaman Vargas, who is still considered to be the greatest healer trained in the highland-Andean tradition of coca divination and healing to have ever lived.

I found myself in this windowless room because the program Dr. Cabieses had envisioned to integrate traditional healers like don Benito into the Peruvian medical system had been indefinitely postponed: "I'm sorry, Mr. Miro-Quesada, we have no money to support you," I had been told. Fieldwork had been cancelled. My hopes of returning to work with don Benito had been thwarted. Instead, I had been shuffled to this thankless assignment for the duration of the time I owed my government. The money had dried up, and I had been cast aside to finish my two-year commitment pushing paper. I had to return to live with my mother, in my childhood home, in order to be able to pay the child support I owed.

I was restless and worried; and I was broke. Could this job pushing paper really be the reason I had been blessed with such success and accomplishment? Was this all that awaited me at the end of all my training?

And what about my promises to don Celso? How could I bring my friends and colleagues from the U.S. to experience the beauty of Peru's wisdom traditions while my country's political climate was deteriorating? With the terror of Shining Path revolutionaries on the rise and news of massacres in Peru's southern Andes no one wanted to travel to Peru now. My dejection deepened as I moved yet another file on my desk between the piles.

This was my situation as I returned to my country after completing my post-graduate fellowship at Emory University at the end of 1982. Let me say at the outset that I am supremely grateful for every one of the difficulties I encountered during this period. I share these with you here because these experiences remind us that life is a great teacher, if we but open ourselves to her lessons. I also choose to share some of the darkest moments in my life to illustrate the power of an open heart as we open more gracefully to a peaceful acceptance of What Is. In the few years following my return from the United States to Lima, I had ample opportunity for growth as I began to cope with the challenges of the wounds of my childhood.

When I was a child, I was convinced that I was cognitively impaired and the worst student in the world. I had the distinction of being dead last in my high school graduating class. "You're not college material, Mr. Miro-Quesada," my high school guidance teacher had told me. So, rather than attempt and fail the entrance exams for any university in Peru, I had traveled to the northeastern U.S. in 1970 to work construction for my maternal uncle Frank. He was known as "Mutt" among his acquaintances, who were also mobster Lucky Luciano's friends.

As I began to make my way in the working world, I had continued apprenticing with don Celso, returning to Peru as frequently as money and time would allow. Along the way, I had also gained confidence as I began navigating the U.S. educational system. After my first "A" since kindergarten while attending night school, I attained an A.S. in Microbiology at a junior college in Connecticut. Afterward, I was accepted at

Duke University, where I earned a B.A. in Psychology. The life-changing experiences I was having with don Celso had made me passionate about the inner workings of the psyche and about the role of spiritual awakening in healing the body, the heart, and the mind.

After finishing at Duke, I had worked for three years as a psychiatric assistant in an intensive care psychiatric ward at Duke Medical Center. Then, I had been accepted to the premiere humanistic psychology program in the country, at what is now the University of West Georgia. While studying there, I had opened a small clinical practice, helping others to grow and heal. Upon graduation, I had applied for and was awarded a prestigious Organization of American States postgraduate fellowship at Emory University in Atlanta.

Around the same time I accepted don Celso's bequest to carry his 3,000-year-old lineage of healing to the peoples of the north, I met Dr. Fernando Cabieses. This internationally respected Peruvian neurosurgeon and visionary was spearheading the integration of traditional and modern medicine in my country. He told me he needed my help. He introduced me to don Benito Corihuaman Vargas in Wasao near Cusco. The plan was that don Benito would participate in that project, which would serve to pay back my obligation to the government of Peru for their investment in my OAS fellowship.

After meeting don Benito, I returned to Atlanta to finish my last semester at Emory University. I was excited and cocky. I got busy with the business of growing up. I had recently married and my first wife and I had a child just as I was about to graduate. Then, my life began to fall apart.

My little girl's mother, suffering from a severe post-partum depression, decided she didn't want to be married anymore. Even though she was emotionally unable to care for our child, she refused to let my daughter travel back to Peru with me. I couldn't stay in the U.S. because of the terms of my OAS fellowship. So I had to return to Peru without my baby girl.

Although a trained clinician, I found myself embodying the neuroses of my own dysfunctional childhood. The pain I harbored as I relived my parents' violence toward one another returned to haunt me as I inhabited the hallways of my childhood home once again. I was consumed by self-loathing as I considered my own failed marriage, my struggle providing for my daughter, and the expectations associated with my Miro-Quesada surname.

I was, after all, Oscar Manuel Miro-Quesada III. I was the grandson of the general director of Peru's premiere newspaper. Among his many and varied accomplishments, my grandfather was the first to translate Einstein's Theory of Relativity into Spanish. He made science accessible to the public, and Einstein himself had thanked him for his work. My father had been minister of education, ambassador to France during the time of Charles de Gaulle, a founding member of the American Academy of Sciences because of his accomplishments as director of Peru's National Health Service, and he had held a government post similar to that of Surgeon General in the United States. I had so much to live up to as the namesake of such great men. It was more than I could bear.

Under the weight of such social expectations, I found refuge and escape in drugs, alcohol, and sex. In order to numb my pain, I acted out. I was arrested on multiple occasions.

My father, increasingly disappointed and concerned with how his highly educated son was adjusting to life in Lima after graduate school, bailed me out repeatedly. My uncle Frank, who was running from his own associations with the mafia in Connecticut, came to live with us. He had settled his giant four-hundred-pound frame into two first-class seats on the trip from New York to Lima. He brought his bodyguards and his lifestyle with him into my mother's home, swaggering and boozing and ranting and renting women by the hour. My godfather also lived with us during a time when his black-market business in women's clothing had turned into something darker—he started dealing drugs. The household became more and more chaotic. I missed don Celso terribly.

One afternoon when I was drunk and acting out, I was taken into custody—again. For my father, this arrest was the final straw. "Damn it all! Leave him in the slammer so he will finally learn something!" I could hear him shouting even as the echo of his footsteps faded from the cellblock where I lay waiting for the key to turn. I couldn't believe my ears. Through all the years of my dysfunctional childhood, he had been my rock. Now even he appeared to be abandoning me. It was one of the lowest points of my life. I was consumed by despair.

When I was finally released, I felt completely lost and useless and alone. I went up to my room and sat staring in the full-length mirror. I looked deeply into my own reflection. I just knew that I was destined to be something greater than the total jerk I had become. I had seen this in the visions the Shining Ones had shared with me, but I didn't have the self-confidence to trust in what I had been shown. I was suffering deeply. My life was just so dark. "What's left?" I despaired.

"Prayer, man," was the response. "This isn't about being delivered by some enlightened being. This is about promising to do something. Get on your knees and pray." So I did. I got on my knees, and I offered my prayers to the ineffable.

I was so raw that I didn't even have to try. I flooded the floor with my tears, and I cried out loud that I just couldn't take it anymore. "Please direct me. I'll do anything you ask! I'll give up drugs, I'll give up booze and work in soup kitchens. Please, I want to serve you. I'll do anything that *You* put in my path if you please provide me with some meaning and purpose for my life." I just collapsed, sobbing, and unburdened all my pain to the unknowable, without boundaries.

Things really started to change for me then. There came into my life a series of what I can only call intercessions, or maybe "heavenly interventions." It was as though I was opening myself to my destiny. All I had needed to do was to completely surrender—and to sincerely ask for help from that place beyond all ego.

Here is just one example of what began to occur in my life after that day on my knees. With my depression still weighing heavily on my shoulders, I took a walk one morning to visit the ancient ruins of the Huaca Pujllana, which were very near my mother's house in Miraflores. This pre-Columbian temple of the 1,500-year-old Rimac/Lima culture had been my place of refuge and of sanctuary as a young boy. I had often gathered from there the potsherds and scraps of 1,500-year-old textiles that littered the ground. Even as a very young child, I found great comfort and connection as I played in the fields of my ancestors.

I would bring these small treasures home and spend hours arranging and re-arranging these relics on the floor of my parents' garage. Where other children played with action figures or Legos or toy cars, imagining their lives as architects or actors or race car drivers, these remnants of old became my armies and my protectors, my castles and my kings.

On this day, I was walking again among the ruins when I spotted a beggar sitting on the ground at the base of the temple, surrounded by piles of books. "Young man, come and sit by me," beckoned the tattered man. He was wearing rags, and his fingernails were long and filthy. I did as he asked. "Hey man, where did you get all these books, anyway?" I asked him. "It's my own personal library," he responded with liquid eyes. "I have a book for you," he told me then as he handed me a copy of P. D. Ouspensky's *The Psychology of Man's Possible Evolution.* "You need to read this." Bewildered, I took the little volume. I didn't recognize the author or the title at the time.

Then he asked me for a scrap of food in exchange for the gift he had given me. I went back to the house, where my mother had just finished preparing a sumptuous feast of pasta with meat sauce and fresh bread for our noon meal. As I ladled the hot food into tins and walked back to where the beggar sat, I kept thinking how odd it was that this smelly old man had crossed my path. I gave him the food and sat silently with him while he ate. As I gathered the containers and walked back home after he finished, I noticed the sidewalk, which had just been washed. There, imprinted in the glistening concrete were odd markings that looked like some kind of ancient Coptic or Cuneiform-type of writing. I felt goose bumps rising on my skin, but I didn't yet understand.

When I got home with the empty containers, I went to my room and began leafing through the book. As I did, the

significance of this gift passed through my body like lightning. The author was G. I. Gurdjieff's most illustrious student. With my background in humanistic psychology and the
human potential movement, I knew of Gurdjieff. As I read
on, I realized with a start that I already knew the principles
of the teachings in this little volume: "You have been sleep-
walking yet you *can* awaken again to know yourself. Take
heart—you *can* re-member. But you need to *do* the work. You
need to look deeply at yourself, to discipline your negative
emotions and quiet yourself. You need to *sacrifice your suffering* and open yourself to *service*." I jumped off the bed and ran
down the stairs. This little man had obviously been an angel
sent to help me understand. When I got back to the ruins,
there was no sign of him anywhere. This little book is the only
evidence I have of that encounter. Yet the story that it tells
became foundational for the development of the Pachakuti
Mesa, which was already gestating in me.

I continued to have experiences that I now realize as
"heavenly interventions" in support of my spiritual development. I knew I needed to get out of that windowless room. I
needed to find a way to return to work with don Benito. But
I had no means or time to do it. Then, out of the blue, I got
an unexpected phone call. It was from the medical director
of Petro-Peru. His name was Dr. Hinostroza, and he was a
beautiful soul. "We've heard wonderful things about you, Dr.
Miro-Quesada," he told me, "and we'd like to offer you a job
coordinating our substance abuse program up in Talara. If
you accept, we'll pay you well, cover your room, board, and
travel expenses, and give you two weeks off every month."
The offer sounded too good to be true. How in the world did
this guy hear about me, I wondered? So I asked my father,

"Hey, Dad, did you hook me up with this guy?" But he didn't know anything about it. It was just so curious.

I took the job. By that time the OAS had told me, "Look, Mr. Miro-Quesada, we don't have the money to pay you for your work, so you are released from your contract with us, and you can work in whatever capacity you want to. As long as you don't leave Peru for the next two years, we will consider your obligation to the state as fulfilled. We are sure that, whatever you do, you will be contributing to the future of the country."

Even though I only had a master's degree, at Petro-Peru they treated me like I was a medical doctor. Struggling with my own addictions, I felt like the most dysfunctional "doctor" on the planet, but they treated me like a savior nonetheless. The program I developed was successful and replicated throughout the country. So I was finally contributing to society. At last I was being of service to those in need.

With the money I saved from my new job, I was able to find myself a little apartment, and I could afford to finance trips to Cusco to visit don Benito. Even though I had only met him once, when Dr. Cabieses introduced him to me the year before, I felt drawn to him. I'd heard stories about don Benito being able to call in the cold winds of the mountain lords called *apus* to clear all types of conditions.

When I found don Benito and presented myself to him, his response was formal and cool. "Why are you here? Who invited you here, anyway?" he asked me in a measured voice. "Don't you remember me, don Benito?" I replied. "I came to visit you last year with Dr. Cabieses." He looked me up and down and said, "Oh yes, I remember. Your hair was longer then, and you didn't wear a tie." I smiled, a little arrogantly, as

I remember. "Well, that's the life I'm living now in Lima, you know," I said, pleased that he remembered me. "You know, I've heard really good things about your work, don Benito, and I'd really like you to show me your traditions. I'd like to learn your ways." He frowned a little. "That's not how it's done," he told me. "I already have my apprentice, and you can't just come calling and insert yourself in this way."

This time, it was my turn to frown. "But, don Benito," I asserted, "let's help each other out. You know my father works in the Ministry of Health. If you help me, if you take me on as your apprentice, perhaps I can help your community in some way. I have my connections in Lima, you know."

"You can hang around if you can find me when you come to call, I guess. But I have business right now up in Q'eros. So

it will have to be another time," was don Benito's response. With that, he turned and went inside. And that's the way it was. The first several times I saw don Benito after that, he just ignored me. But there was a kind of twinkle in his eye when he spoke to me, and I remember just falling in love with this gentle man. So I kept returning and hoping his feelings toward me would change.

I would arrive in Cusco and go directly to Wasao, where I would ask after him. "He's not here, but you can wait if you want." This was the answer I always received. And so I would wait. All day. In the evening I would return to Cusco just to sleep. The next day I would try again. And I would wait again, in vain. After a week of waiting, I would have to return to Lima, in order to head back up to Talara. A fortnight later, I would repeat the process. This went on for months.

"He's just testing me," I remember telling myself one day as I reflected on the kinds of teachings that don Celso had set before me. I thought myself worthy of these challenges and was determined to succeed, so I kept returning. Now, in looking back, I realize he didn't care one way or the other if I showed up or if I didn't. I was nothing to him at all because I had not yet learned the laws of sacred reciprocity and importance of *ayni*.

The next time I had to leave Cusco for Talara, I decided to drive instead of flying. I wanted to stop at the 3,000-year-old ruins of Chavín de Huantar, which was the birthplace of the *kamasqa* healing tradition I had apprenticed to with don Celso. This Chavín temple outside the mountain town of Huaraz was considered to be the cradle of north Peruvian *curanderismo*. Don Celso had always wanted to come here with me so that I could sleep with my head against the stone etching that depicted the 3,000-year-old winged-jaguar-shaman who held the sacred medicine cactus in his claws. I was at a loss to understand why my work with don Benito was not progressing as I had hoped. I deeply wanted to apprentice with him, but I felt thwarted at every turn. If don Celso had still been around, I would have asked his help to understand. But he was gone now, and I needed some direction. I decided to ask for help by going directly to the source.

In those days, there were no guards to keep people out of the ruins after hours. So I just took my backpack into the ruins to sleep under the stars as close as I could get to the etching. As I looked up into the night sky, the Milky Way above my head was incredibly bright and near. The Pleiades and Orion were clearly visible in the night sky. As I looked up, I remember feeling that this is exactly who I really am. This is it. I AM.

As I began to doze, I started to see these images. At first they looked like they were rooftops in an old medieval European village. Then those rooftops changed to *malocas*. All of a sudden, there were round stone buildings with straw roofs, and I found myself in Kuelap. I didn't even know at the time that this place existed, even though I had heard of the Chachapoyas culture. But there I was. I started to remember. I thought to myself, oh my God, I haven't visited this place in a long, long time and so I went deeper into sleep. I started to dream.

In my dream, I was back at Chavín de Huantar. It was at the height of its glory as a temple and pilgrimage site. I was a high priest coordinating ritual sacrifices to the fifteen-foot-tall etched stone god known today as the *lanzón*. I was letting llama blood drip over the huge stone as well as offerings of cornmeal, coca leaves, and ground-up sea shells.

Bringing these offerings to me were pilgrims, coming from the four directions. There were caravans of these pilgrims all coming with pack animals—with llamas and alpacas—lumbering under the weight of all the offerings that they carried. These offerings from every region of Peru—from the coast and highlands and the jungles to the east—were all being brought to the temple to be given to the priests. And I remember being with a group of initiates at the entrance to the temple on the north side. There, a group of people was receiving the bundles, receiving the animals, placing them in a storage area, and allowing the pilgrims to come into the temple. We were all dressed very plainly.

And as the dream continued, I remember understanding that the people who were coming last into the temple site were sick and tired and old. There was a special place for them in the temple where they were welcomed. I knew that these faithful pilgrims would return to their homelands with an escort of healthier young men who had been prepared by those of us residing permanently at Chavín to accompany them. These escorts would carry with them a measure of the food and provisions that had been brought into the temple by those whose harvests had been abundant. And so the people who didn't have anything to offer returned to their places with riches that came from those who had journeyed to the temple to give. There were no questions asked; this was just what was done.

I awoke from my dream. The principle of sacred reciprocity that was practiced by my ancestors had deeply imprinted itself upon me in that experience. Giving and receiving, without condition, was the key to sacred relationship. Service to one's brothers and one's sisters whether from down the street or across the universe was all that was required. That's what my visit to Chavín did for me.

My next trip to visit don Benito came after this realization. I arrived at his home carrying offerings of many kinds for don Benito and his family. I knew not to take him the local corn-beer Quechua speakers call *chicha*, even though he loved to drink it, because his wife Natalia was known by everyone in the village as the best *chicha*-maker around. "You are wise not to bring me *chicha*," he told me with a twinkle in his eye.

"Because if you had, I would have thrown it to the pigs rather than drinking it myself." In being sensitive to him and to his family, and in being kind, I finally began to win his respect. It was only when he began to recognize me as someone who could embody the loving kindness of *munay*—which is more than anything a *feeling* of deep compassion—that he began to respond to me.

Even so, he made me jump through a lot of hoops as his apprentice. He would send me on long and arduous pilgrimages to all the mountains in the area—to call upon the *apus* and to make ritual offerings to them. "Oscar, go out to the base of mount Pachatusan with your coca leaf *kintus* and your *chicha*. Go out and practice your *haywas*, which are prayer-filled offerings to all the powers of the natural world. I'll be along to pick you up and bring you back in just a little while," he would tell me. And so I would go and make my offerings. And I would wait for him to come and get me. And he never did. And I would find my way at the end of the day back to his house only to find him drinking *chicha* with his buddies. He never had any intention of coming to collect me! He had a lot of fun with me at my expense. But I also understand that he was testing my sincerity and my resolve. He was making sure that I really understood what it means to give for the sake of giving rather than because I expected something in return.

The day I finally understood how *ayni* or sacred reciprocity is at the core of all healing, don Benito had asked me to assist him with a patient. He was doing a disease "extraction" with a guinea pig. He asked me to bathe the guinea pig in cold, cold water before he used the animal in his healing ceremony. And as he rubbed the guinea pig over the body of the patient to extract the disease, he whispered his prayers of gratitude to his mountain allies, to all the *apus* of the region.

Then he told me, "Go and offer this coca leaf to the river in whose water you bathed this guinea pig. And go and offer this little drink to the river too." He had me running back and forth like that, and I realized that reciprocity is about returning offerings to the source of healing and reverently honoring all the beings that are really behind everything. The guinea pig, the water that was used to bathe the guinea pig, the mountains from which the water flows, the coca leaf *kintu* that is the vehicle for prayer, don Benito, and myself: We are all in this interdependent web, and the *paqokuna* tradition is all about honoring these relationships. And that is a beautiful thing.

Finally one day, not too long before he died, don Benito told me I had watched him make his prayerful offerings to the *apus* long enough. He wanted to teach me how to make a proper *despacho*. *Despachos* are ritual offering-packets that are created in beautifully intricate mandala-like shapes where every single offering item has both a particular placement and a symbolic meaning. These are filled with coca leaf *kintus* and beans and corn and candy and llama fat and all the other offerings traditionally given to the *apus*. He didn't call them *despachos*, though. Instead, he called them *haywas*. With this name, he emphasized that these bundles were prayerful *offerings* of one's self acting in alliance and sacred relationship with all the energies and powers of the natural world.

And so we were sitting on these two stumps, and he said, "We're going to make a prayer so you can really learn how to do this. Watch me, but even more than that, listen to the sound of my breath as I blow my kiss into this little coca *kintu*." And so he began.

As I watched, I found myself so focused on the ritual operation, on the configuration of the offerings that he was putting together, that I was forgetting to listen to the sound of don Benito's prayers. I was obsessed with the ritual acts rather than allowing myself to really "live the spirit."

So there I was trying to replicate what he was doing and every time I would place a *kintu* down, I noticed that don Benito would grimace. He didn't say anything at all, but he would wince. And when I was done preparing the offering bundle, he would say, "No, that's not right" and have me start again. And I would do it again, and again, and again, and it still wasn't right.

Finally, I got fed up with focusing on the proper placement of the ingredients, and I found myself spending much more time breathing on the leaf and communing with the spirit of the place. When I did, I found myself moving into a place where there was no time—just an eternal present moment. Because really entering into a loving relationship has nothing to do with how good of a performer you are. It has to do with entering into a conversation with the *apus* as you pray. It's about how you actually picture yourself walking and deeply interacting with the place. If the ritual operation is not infused with that spirit of relationship, it is just empty. But when the prayers are given with the attention and care that any loving relationship deserves, when you actually travel to visit and to deeply commune—listening for the answers as well as speaking from the heart—it doesn't matter what the offering bundle looks like at all. Once I really gave the *art* of relationship my focus and began to commune with the *apus*, don Benito smiled and said, "Yes that's how it's done." That's what he was trying to teach all along.

Ritual Begets Relationship

To harness the spiritual power of creation, as did our ancestral peoples, we need to return to a deep understanding of how sacred relationship works. "Feed the earth first and then you will have the strength to go out on the healing path," don Benito taught me. The more loving the energy that we can generate as we attend to these earth-honoring ceremonies, the quicker the transmutation of our physical, mental, emotional, and spiritual bodies occurs.

The core of what don Benito taught me, even as I was struggling with my own insecurities, is this: By doing earth-healing rites and ceremonies, we reestablish a conscious, awakened, sacred relationship with the Earth. This encourages all the conscious beings who inhabit our beloved *Pachamama* to feel more comfortable revealing themselves to nurture and support us. This is the nature of *ayni*.

Through ritual action we restore harmonious relationships both "within and without," for these are the same. By focusing on service to our beloved Earth mother, we open ourselves to receive love and comfort from powers that are far older and wiser than is any human relative. As don Benito told me, "These *apus*, these mountain lords have been around a very long time. They've seen people come and go for millennia. They have witnessed many, many things. Take the time to enter into a true living spirit relationship with the place and they will sustain you. That's how they work."

It is not uncommon to suffer because our primary caregivers were unable to instill the deep sense of worth, trust, and belonging that every being deserves to feel. Yet by engaging in ritual practices that call upon our Mother Earth, we can finally quiet the erroneous messages of loathing and lack we internalized as children. We can separate ourselves from the negative stories we were told that we have internalized. Through ritual, we can recognize our essential nature as we deepen our honoring relationships with the natural world.

You see, as we participate in actions of kindness and service to the mother of us all, we wrap ourselves in gratitude. We receive as we give. We reclaim our intrinsic worth. We no longer need validation, nor do we need to fear rejection. Healing is as simple as this: As we walk in beauty, we *are* beauty.

Through participation in earth-honoring ceremonies we are able to shift from fear to love, from desire to grateful acceptance of "what is," and from separation to wholeness. Through ritual offerings of gratitude, we beget new relationships of love, care, and compassion with ourselves, with others, and with the world. As we reclaim the deep understanding of our birthright, we naturally pay it forward into the world. Thus, *ritual begets relationship* and sanctifies a new pattern of being. As we embody the principle of *ayni* in All Our Relations, we align with the magnificence of who we truly are.

This is how all spiritually attuned civilizations on this planet have lived. The Sumerians, Egyptians, and ancient Vedic peoples as well as the ancestral civilizations of the Americas were all attuned to this truth. Ritual action begets relationship, and this right action heals even the deepest wounds. As we re-enact the earth-honoring rituals in ways akin to what they did, we can lovingly influence the emergence of a global reality in which we want to live.

Thoughts, words, deeds—these are the tools we have been given to restore harmony in the world. Yet when right thought and right speech is impossible to project because of how we feel about ourselves, ritual action is the surest way to reclaim our deepest knowing of our worth. Don Benito showed me this through his gentle example. The ritual gesture of composing graceful ceremony is the way we re-member ourselves as an interdependent strand within the sacred web of life. This is the way we bring beauty into our hearts. It is how we open our hearts fully to love. This was don Benito's greatest teaching of all.

This wisdom of teaching love by the way we live in sacred reciprocity is the ritual foundation of the Pachakuti Mesa Tradition. As Mesa carriers—as practitioners of this tradition—we recognize that we are an integral part of the intricate web of interdependence that powers physical and spiritual worlds. In these rituals, we honor all the beings with whom we share this plane, this space/time, this consciousness, what Quechua speakers call *pacha*. Through these ritual arts, we come into deeper awareness that our right action heals the world.

As we compose our rituals, we re-member our interdependence with the ground below, the sky above, the inner world of our deepest feelings as well as outer worlds of thought, word, and action. Through artfully structuring the sacred space of our mesa-grounds as well as gracefully restructuring cosmic order through our actions, we co-create a conscious "turning over"—a *kuti*—of the way relationship between spirit and matter is understood. As we become more adept in our relationship with the shamanic powers and forces revealed through our Pachakuti Mesa ground, we also contribute to the prophesied completion of the current *pachakuti* that my ancestors spoke of. We reclaim our role as co-creators of the New Earth.

One might say that the Pachakuti Mesa is a reflection of both our highest selves and our fondest dreams for the world. As the magic of the Pachakuti Mesa is witnessed, appreciated, and harnessed, our soul remembers, spirit awakens, heart leaps, mind knows, and body follows. Our wholeness is remembered and sacred relationship is restored.

Practices for Opening Heart: Composing Rituals of Sacred Relationship

Sanctifying Your Space

The medicine pieces that were gathered ceremonially as described in the last chapter hold particular archetypal forms, energies, and healing power. As you artfully arrange these on a sacred cloth that will serve as the altar ground of your Pachakuti Mesa, you foster an experience of interpersonal wholeness and transpersonal harmony with Mother Earth.

To begin the process of constructing the Pachakuti Mesa, find a pristine space within your homes or workplaces that can be set aside as an aesthetically beautiful sanctuary for healing, meditation, and personal renewal. Position the altar according to the cardinal directions so that the organization of pieces on the mesa reflects the implicit order of the natural world. Ideally, you should lay the mesa according to the cardinal directions, so that the "open end," or the side closest to you, faces south while the north side of the mesa lies snug against a window or a wall. Choose a beautiful *unkhuña*—a hand woven Andean *manta* or a similarly special textile—as the base upon which all your sacred items will rest. Even the ground cloth that you choose is special because it embodies the understanding that the web of life in which we all live is process and product, warp and weft, cultural "tradition" and individual choice. The web of life in which we all partici-pate carries all these threads and is made beautiful by all these dynamics.

Before laying the altar cloth, it is important to consecrate the ground that will hold your Pachakuti Mesa. To do this, use offerings that reflect the most sacred medicines of the Americas. These are blue cornmeal, tobacco, coca leaves, and Florida Water.

As don Benito taught me, it is not operation that is most important when composing ritual. Instead, it is the quality of the *haywa*, which is your prayer. Thus, remember to center yourself first, as you learned in chapter 1, deeply communing with your soul-nature. Then consecrate yourself again—in this perfect, present moment—as a pristine vehicle, as spirit having an embodied physical experience. In doing this, you consciously bring spirit into material form.

After communing and consecrating in this way, begin your consecration of the ground on which you will lay your altar cloth with Florida Water—this thirst-quenching elixir of living water has a scent that helps us remember the Eternal Now we inhabited as souls before our present incarnation. Your use of a single drop of Florida Water to open sacred space expresses your reverence for and your commitment of service to the earth.

After placing a drop of Florida Water on the ground, take a small handful of blue cornmeal and gently kiss it with your prayers of unity and of surrender to the cycles of becoming that carry us through life. Beginning in the south, at the point closest to where you are sitting, place a perfect circle of blue cornmeal clockwise around the single drop of Florida Water to embody the unbroken, interdependent circle of life in which we all participate. We are all part of that circle, whose center is everywhere and whose circumference is nowhere.

Next, place an equilateral cross of loose-leaf tobacco, from north to south and from east to west. As you do, reflect upon your commitment to bring spirit into matter from the first dawn to the last sunset of your earthly incarnation. Next, make a *kintu* of three perfect coca leaves—or bay leaves if this most sacred medicine plant is unavailable—and gently blow your prayers into these, just as don Benito taught me. Then place the *kintu* on top of the other offerings and lovingly cover these with the sacred cloth that will serve as the ground of your Pachakuti Mesa.

Placing and Empowering the Directional Pieces of the Pachakuti Mesa

On the Pachakuti Mesa altar cloth, you will lay your medicine pieces in a specific mandala-like pattern that is more akin to a Fibonacci spiral than it is to a medicine wheel. The direction of the south (that which is closest to the practitioner) is the place of *Pachamama*, who is our beloved Earth mother. The most appropriate medicine piece to embody her solid, foundational energy, the industriousness of right action—*llankay*—that nurtures and sustains all life, is a gift from the earth herself. This may be a stone or a crystal.

Moving in a clockwise direction around the perimeter of the mesa, we come to the west, which is the place of our beloved *Mamakilla*, who is our Mother Moon. She is the Queen of Heaven, the mother of all cycles and all that ebbs and flows. She is the eternal circle that is life. A shell or a small bowl filled with pure water which embodies compassion and the deep feeling of *munay* is the most recommended medicine piece to hold the archetypal energies of the West.

In the Pachakuti Mesa Tradition, the north embodies the energies of the highest celestial realms, which lie beyond our powers of comprehension. This is the realm of the Great Originating Mystery—*Wiracocha.* It is the rarified abode of the sacred Wind of Creation, the place of spirit. It is also the place of re-membering, which Quechua speakers call *yuyay.* The medicine item you will lay in the north is the finger that points to the crack between the worlds: it is the message and the messenger. So it is appropriate to place the feathers of our winged relatives there—those who soar to the highest realms.

In the Pachakuti Mesa Tradition, east is the abode of *Inti,* who is Father Sun, from whose orb life-affirming light is cast upon the earth every day. It is the seat of wisdom—*yachay*— teachings both for and of the illumined mind. A candle— symbol of vibratory quickening—is placed in the east to awaken our awareness of connection to a Higher Truth.

After placing your pieces in south, west, north, and east, respectively, you ceremonially anchor your mesa ground as you place the *misarumi*—the center piece—remaining conscious that the mesa is a dynamic, evolving spiral rather than a "medicine wheel." This anchor, which is called *K'uychi,* or Sacred Rainbow, houses the unifying essence of our sacred rainbow body. Through this ritual gesture, we align with our soul's spiral progression into ever more refined states of being. As the soul evolves, we spiral ever inward toward the center of our lives as living portals between all worlds. So in the center of your altar cloth, you place a medicine piece that is the most beautiful, meaningful, and most elevated reflection of your essential self, which is your soul. This self-awakened soul is blessed by the perfection of the present moment and joyously celebrates its sacred relationship with all beings. This is self as Unity—which Quechua speakers call *huñuy*. From this center of our being unfolds unlimited co-creative energy throughout the spiral of our becoming.

Basic Pachakuti Mesa Configuration

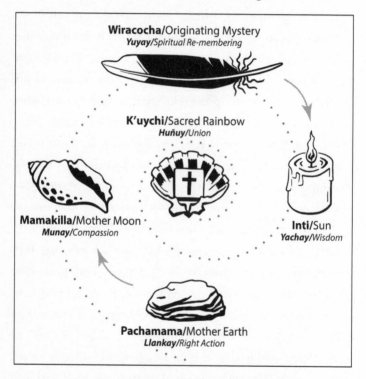

"Right action, borne of compassionate spiritual wisdom, unites."

To empower each of these pieces with these energies, you simply pick them up one by one, placing them in your right hand with your left hand open to the heavens, and tone their respective names seven times each. To do this, start in the south and move always clockwise around the mesa until ending in the center. Take your time with each piece, reflecting on the most elevated feeling-state you can call into your hearts that most reflects your living relationship with *Pachamama,* with *Mamakilla,* with *Wiracocha,* with *Inti,* and with *K'uychi.* Make the journey into the heart of each of these relationships, calling forth the most beautiful images you can visualize for each of these powers. *Feel* their radiance. Reflect on a time in your life when you radiated each of the attributes embodied in these archetypes: When you felt physically, emotionally, spiritually, and mentally at one with their power. Then and only then do you tone their names and call their attributes into the pieces that have been lovingly gathered to hold their energies.

The toning is done by using a two-pitch cadence for each directional word. The sounds of each syllable of *Pachamama,* for example, are drawn out like this: paaaaach-aaa-maaaaa-maaaaa. The first three syllables are toned to the sound of E above middle C. For the last syllable, allow this to slide down a note to D above middle C. This is repeated three times. Then pause and feel, giving gratitude for the arrival of the power and the consciousness associated with our beloved Earth mother, *Pachamama.*

You then repeat exactly the same process, and the same toning, with the name *Mamakilla,* which becomes maaaaa-maaaaa-kiiiii-lllllaaaa as you tone. Again, after completing toning the name three times, pause and feel the resonance as you become aligned and attuned to the energies of our dear *Mamakilla,* Mother Moon. Moving to the north, do the same thing for *Wiracocha* so that this becomes wiiiii-raaaa-coch-aaaaa. Pause and feel.

Next, tone *Inti* three times. In the case of this name, which has only two syllables, elongate the syllables to match the tones so that you slide from the E above middle C to the D as you tone "nnnnnn," and then "tiii" is toned on the D pitch. Again, pause and feel.

Finally, repeat the same two-syllable version of this toning process invoking the name of *K'uychi,* just as you did for *Inti,* with the exception that the *pitch* for this toning is raised so that instead of beginning on the E above middle C and sliding down one note, you begin on the A above middle C and slide to G with the syllable that begins with "—chi."

This is the way that you empower your medicine pieces. After this ritual empowerment, open your mesa by toning these directions, three times each, as you direct your loving intention toward the center of your mesa with both hands. As a reminder that your mesa is now awake and ready to receive your offerings of gratitude as well as to serve you, light the candle that you have placed in the east. As you do these things, you foster an experience of interpersonal wholeness and transpersonal harmony with Mother Earth. And this deepened experiential awareness of your interdependence with both seen and unseen dimensions of life provides a tangible foundation for the emergence of a heartfelt, earth-honoring, sacred community among all those who come into your lives. Constructing and opening your mesas is a beautiful way to compose the kind of ritual that will open your hearts and lead you home again to love.

CHAPTER 4

TRANSFORMING MIND/THE ART OF CONNECTING TO OUR SOURCE

The Great Work is not so much about changing the world as it is about changing oneself in the process. One's greatest gift to humanity is being free of oneself.

The Challenge of Transforming Mind: How Can We Quiet the Chatter of Our "Ego-Minds" to Discover Both Purpose and Power?

She hums while driving down Main Street having just purchased a gift for her husband. Suddenly, a man cuts sharply in front of her, nearly clipping the fender of her car. She honks and curses loudly. Changing lanes, she speeds past him with middle-finger extended. He returns the gesture. "Happy holidays, moron!" she shouts, the blood rushing into her face. Road-rage trumping all logic, the wounded ego has reacted— again. What makes us such slaves to circumstance?

As Pachakuti Mesa Tradition practitioners, we celebrate the primacy of consciousness and the unlimited power of the human psyche. We acknowledge the undisputed wisdom of the first universal law that "All is *MIND*." We recognize matter as *effect*, rather than as *cause*. We are confident that if we can first shape it in our mind, through disciplined imagination and intention, we *will* find it in our lives!

Yet, all too often, we confuse thought with "thinking." When we do, we are inundated with cacophonous chatter. This is the "chatter" of our ego-mind (sometimes called our "monkey-mind"). When we confuse the chatter of our ego with the "Mind" that the Thrice Great Hermes spoke of, we find our best intentions to be thoughtful—or mindful—betrayed!

So the challenge for this chapter is this: How can we discipline our thoughts and find calm and balance and gratitude? How can we learn to quiet the chatter of our "monkey-mind" so that we can hear the quiet voice of our inner wisdom and reconnect to Source?

Ironically, the first step toward this mastery requires us to let go of our need to be masters. It requires surrendering "willful" control to a power much greater than we can possibly envision. "Transforming the monkey-mind" is about trusting and honoring and opening up to the unknown as we surrender to un-knowing. As we do, we begin to more easily discern the wisdom of that Native American prayer that beseeches us to know the difference between that which *is* and that which we are called to *change*. As we willingly surrender control, we burn away the ego, freeing ourselves in new ways. As we continue to surrender—again and again (for awakening to consciousness is a process), we align ourselves with higher and deeper levels of being, connecting deeply, and becoming one with love.

My Encounter with Our Star Relatives: Break-Down as Break-Through

During the years after completing my studies in the United States in 1982 I experienced a real *dark night of the soul*. It was a time of shamanic dismemberment, where everything that I thought "real" was just stripped away. Like most shamanic apprentices, I was taken to the brink of complete annihilation as a prerequisite to being able to serve others. This was the period when I was studying with don Benito, who crossed over in 1986. It was the period when I was working with Petro-Peru up north in Talara and still struggling with my own addictions. I have already spoken of some of the synchronicities that began occurring after falling on my knees and begging to be shown my greater purpose in life. Well, these synchronicities just got more and more bizarre as time went on.

Since the moment I offered myself in service that day, it appeared that I had received a powerful, if dangerous gift. Like the young "sorcerer's apprentice" in the classic film *Fantasia,* it seemed I had suddenly gained special powers. As unlikely as it sounds, from the moment I had pleaded to the universe for meaning and direction as I collapsed in my room before that full-length mirror, it appeared as though I had an ever-increasing capacity to manifest whatever thoughts I held in my mind!

At first, these untamed psychic powers appeared as harmless allies and so I played with them quite innocently. One day while sitting in a crowd of people, I began to envision a comedic situation. As I looked around, everyone around me was laughing, even though there was nothing particularly funny going on, except in my mind. Another time that I projected my thoughts out into the world only to have these mirrored back was when I was sitting in a movie theater. The film was one of those roll-on-the-floor-laughing kinds of comedies and everyone in the audience was clearly enjoying it immensely. As a test, I conjured up a very sad thought and suddenly I heard people near me crying. It was powerfully disconcerting and yet it was seductively empowering too. But like the young apprentice in the Disney classic, I was not yet prepared to deal responsibly with that gift.

My relationship with my Lima girlfriend was deteriorating. One day I learned that she had been cheating on me. I confronted her. She denied it. Then I saw her with my own eyes. She was in a three-way tryst with her stepfather and stepbrother. Not only was I witnessing an orgy, but I was seeing the most debasing kind of incest that I could possibly imagine.

I confronted the three of them, but they all denied it! They told me I was delusional and paranoid. It seemed so far-fetched I began to wonder if I could believe my own eyes or not. Yet I also was so incensed at her lies and deceit that for three days straight, I prayed. I said, "If this is truly happening, I need *proof* so that these sons of bitches stop telling me that I'm hallucinating!" I said, "If she is really cheating on me then let her develop a vaginal condition such that she can't have sex with *anyone.*" And it happened. Just like that. I was a free radical in the playground of the gods!

Soon after, while still reeling from the implications of my own power, I came upon my mother standing in the kitchen. She smelled of sulfur and as I looked at her, horns started growing out of her head! My own head was spinning and I started to sweat. I wasn't in control of what was manifesting at all. "This has to stop," I cried silently. But there was a voice inside me saying, "No! This is the consequence of your evil living, of what you did to this woman just for your own ego gratification!" And then the voice said, "That's nothing. Go outside in the back yard and look what happens next."

So I went outside. The house was on a very small corner lot with just a bit of grass, but my mother had put all her creative energy into planting beautiful flowers there. There were roses and *floripondio* trees and bamboos and many other varieties of plants. As I looked, all of a sudden, all of the plants start to wilt. Literally! Then, the sky got very, very black. It looked just like ink. I was terrified.

The next morning, convinced that I had been hallucinating after all, I got up and went outside. All of the leaves, all of the flowers were just lying on the ground, withered and completely dry. As I walked in the garden, the foliage just turned to dust under my feet. I felt totally out of control. My mind was flooded by psychoid-archetypal powers that were becoming immediately externalized as my surrounding reality. I experienced anger, fear, and paranoia. My unresolved shadow-self was being expressed beyond thought. I was on the verge of madness. I needed help!

In the middle of this intense craziness, I was lying on my bed one day in complete anguish about these occurrences when a bright light shot in through my window. My heart began to race as I suddenly remembered an earlier time, when I was nine. Back then, a mind-shattering collective experience of extraterrestrial intelligence had provided a catalyst for my awakening. It was a moment in time when the veil between worlds thins and what is normally unseen becomes visible to all.

It had been a typical late Sunday afternoon in my neighborhood, when parents would stand outside their homes and chat with one another while children played. On that day the sky started to darken, unexpectedly. It became a deep purple-violet, just like the darkest part of a solar eclipse. There was this uncanny silence too. You couldn't hear a sound anywhere—not even that of your own breath. It was like being in a parallel universe!

All of a sudden, a huge orb appeared in the sky above us. It was a perfect sphere of brilliant white light that seemed as large as the full moon. As more than twenty of my neighbors all lifted their eyes in open-mouthed wonder, this light started to bounce across the sky. It was just like the bouncing ball in one of those sing-a-long cartoons we used to watch on the television as kids. Then, as suddenly as it had appeared, it just vanished—right out of the middle of the sky! Afterward, no one spoke a word. Instead, everybody just put their heads down, turned around and walked into their homes. And no one spoke a word about what had happened.

That same night, I was in my room. I was reading my favorite little *El Condorito* comic book to help me relax. Suddenly, a beam of light shone in through my bedroom window. It flashed on the empty pale green wall across from my bed like a floodlight, illuminating everything. It remained there for a long time. Then, just as suddenly as it had come, it disappeared. When I was finally able to get my arms and legs to move, I ran to the window, but nothing was there.

Now the same light was once again shining into the bedroom where I had spent my youth. I leapt to the window and saw the same orb I had seen as a child. Only this time, the light it projected just shot right through me. Then it started to move around the room, like a laser beam, shining here and there, and then right out the door into the hallway as if it was beckoning me and pointing to some place outside my bedroom. I began following the light. As I did, it bent around a corner and moved down the hall. It moved past my mother's bedroom door to the next room where she kept the ironing board and her sewing. It bent around that doorway too and settled on a high cabinet that she used for storage. It stopped there, making a pulsing kind of noise. I climbed on a chair, opened the cabinet and pulled out a photo where the tip of the laser beam now rested. It was a photo of my first guru.

During my early days in the United States, I had been very interested in Eastern religions. At the time, Maharaj Ji, whose advisors had founded the Divine Light Mission in India, was teaching up and down the East Coast. As somewhat of a gnostic myself, I resonated with the guru's teachings that one's need for fulfillment could be satisfied by turning within. Rather than preaching any kind of dogma, he advocated that the source for real peace and joy lies inside. Maharaj Ji was six years younger than I was and really popular with the youth. He was sheer love and joy and playfulness. He was such a pure soul!

So I followed the young avatar around as much as my job and my school schedule would allow. I would hang out at the ashram where he taught and then go on the road to hear him: I went from New London to Hartford to New York and even to Philadelphia, where I was finally initiated into the Mission by one of the guru's more famous devotees—none other than Rennie Davis of the Chicago Seven! Those were radical times.

In the intervening years from the 1970s, when I must have carried the photo with me back to Lima, until that afternoon when this strange light led me to the storage room, the guru had married and his work with the organization had waned. The Divine Light Mission had changed, and I had moved on as well. Now I looked at the photo in wonder. I had completely forgotten about it, but here it was, being shown to me in an hour of need.

Yet it wasn't just the photo that I was being shown by this strange beam of light. When I picked it up, a little pamphlet fell out. "How in the world, did *that* get in here?" I wondered. The laser beam just switched "off" in that moment. I took the little pamphlet back to my room and began reading.

The pamphlet was one of the first publications of Sixto Paz Wells, a Lima native who had founded a civic association in Lima to share his experiences as a human "contactee" back in 1974, when he was just sixteen years old. On the night of his first contact with extraterrestrials, Sixto had been practicing psychographic writing in his Lima home. Suddenly, he began "downloading" messages from a group of star-beings who had been waiting to contact him. According to what was being shared with Sixto, these guides collectively referred to themselves as being part of something called the RAMA Mission. Soon after, Sixto and several of his school friends were instructed to travel to the Chilca desert south of Lima for a face-to-face meeting with these beings. When they did, a hamburger-shaped, metallic craft emitting orange, blue, and yellow light appeared right before their eyes as confirmation that the channeling he had done was very real, indeed! They were shocked and began to panic as the craft hovered less than 300 feet overhead. As their emotions surged, the craft disappeared as quickly as it had arrived. The youth were telepathically informed that the fear they expressed was too dense a vibration to sustain contact with these beings from another dimension. They would have to learn to control their emotions and prepare themselves carefully if they wanted any "close encounter of the third kind."

Over time, Sixto and his friends continued his telepathic communication with these star-beings. As they learned to discipline their minds and to control their emotions, they began interacting with these beings more closely. On several occasions they were informed that UFO's would be waiting for them in the desert at specific times and they had various physical encounters with these. Through a kind of inter-dimensional portal called a "Xendra," Sixto was even able to board their star ships and converse with these extraterrestrial beings. During these meetings, he learned that these beings came from many star systems, but were joined together for a single purpose. They referred to themselves as our "elder brothers." They had a base on Ganymede, which is one of Jupiter's moons, and had been chosen by their respective governments to participate in a mission to help earthly beings awaken to our true power as channels of love and light. Their mission was to assist humans in bringing the light of cosmic consciousness—what we might call "God Consciousness" to Earth.

As I devoured this little pamphlet and considered its message, I was hooked. Sixto talked about disciplining the ego-mind in order to prepare for these encounters and I wanted to learn how to do this. I set out to find Sixto for another reason too. Because he had been contacted by extraterrestrials, I hoped he could help me understand what I had experienced back when I was nine and again on the day when that beam of light had led me straight to the story of the RAMA Mission. I needed some answers, and I knew I was being led to Sixto Paz Wells!

The pamphlet had been mimeographed and distributed back in 1974. By the time I had been led to read it in my mother's sewing room in 1982, Sixto had become very famous. He had many apprentices who were teaching the twenty-two RAMA practices that would help sufficiently raise our "vibration" enough to make contact with the extraterrestrial guides—as well as with our higher selves. RAMA study groups were springing up all over Peru. Sixto was busy and a very hard man to track down. I had traveled all over the coast of Peru—from Tacna to Trujillo—just trying to catch up with him. Eventually, though, I was able to attend a meeting about the RAMA Mission that Sixto himself was facilitating. It was to be held right near my house in the Lima district of Miraflores.

On that night, Sixto was going to be introducing the Mission to a general audience. I took a moment before the presentation to introduce myself. "Hello, Sixto," I started, "I've been looking for you all over Peru. I even went to Tacna to try to interact with you. I'm so glad to finally meet you."

Sixto smiled and responded simply, "Plans change, my dear brother, but we've been waiting for you. Our elder brothers have told me a number of things about you." I knew that the "elder brothers" were how the extraterrestrials referred to themselves. I was intrigued. "What kinds of things have you heard?" I asked. "Well, among other things, they've told me that you have had several near-death experiences. You were visited by three Shining Ones when you were ten. They cured you of your asthma. I've also been told you have suffered a lot because of your parents' very difficult marriage and breakup."

I was so stunned that I began stammering then. He spoke as though he was just commenting on my hair color or my height rather than revealing the deepest secrets and most meaningful events of my life. I knew every single event he mentioned to be absolutely true. As words continued to fail me, he continued, "Well then, welcome and please have a seat. We'll begin the presentation in just a moment." I began seriously questioning my reality then. "Where am I? Who is this guy? Can this really happening to me?" I asked.

I sat down and began listening to his lecture. Sixto was somewhere behind me in the room, advancing slides through a slide projector as he spoke. He told the audience of the long history of contact between star nations and our planet. These included beings from planets within Orion, the Pleiades, Canis Major, and Cygnus. He spoke of intergalactic wars and lost continents, star-nation invaders and instructors, an etheric Shambhala and the "seeding" of species. He spoke of spiritual, mental, and physical universes and a great cosmic plan of awakening. In the slides, there were depictions of intergalactic beings appearing to Isaiah and Ezekiel as Biblical angels. There were artistically rendered illustrations of RAMA guides with whom he had interacted most frequently. There were depictions of a place called the "Crystal City" on Ganymede with gleaming temples where residents from multiple star systems lived together in perfect harmony following a moral code that affirmed Christ Consciousness, which is the recognition that we carry the divine within. They also emphasized heart-derived wisdom, intuitive vision, and peaceful cooperation among all species. It was awe-inspiring and completely different than any planetary history I had been taught in school. As the story continued to unfold on the screen at the front of the room, it all began to feel so familiar, "Oh, that's right. Oh, those were the good old days," I found myself thinking. I remembered being a member of this elevated, otherworldly family in another time.

As I turned my attention again to Sixto's words, I heard him explaining that elder brothers from the RAMA Mission had been drawn to our planetary system because they were extremely concerned about the proliferation of atomic weapons on earth during the decades after World War II. A review of our planetary history had revealed that while free will is necessary to reach the highest plane of soul-evolution possible, this also has dire consequences when misused. Because the ego-mind is borne from the *illusion* of separation from Source—and from love—ego had used our free will to compensate, seeking desperately after that which we believed lost. In this struggle, choosing to seek domination over our planet had become ego's chief comfort. Our free will had become confused with being "in control," and this was leading us down a path of complete estrangement with the sacred dimensions of life. This was a path of perdition.

According to Sixto, our greatest challenge as human beings was to reclaim our essential nature as Christ Consciousness borne of the One Source and to help others to realize this nature in themselves. Thus, the main objective of the RAMA guides was contact with oneself. Our experience of visitation by extraterrestrial intelligences was secondary to the encounter with the Christ Consciousness that is our true essence.

The RAMA guides offered Sixto an opportunity to become their messenger. Their intentions were to advise and to be of service so that human free will became a proper expression of Divine Will.

The name RAMA was significant because RA means "sun" and MA means "earth." Thus RAMA stood for "sun on earth, or light on the third dimension." To become this light—to be illumined—the guides informed us, we must train our mind to become our servant rather than our master. We must develop mindfulness, borne of an open heart. Sixto summarized the message of these RAMA guides as follows: *solo hay*

un momento para amar, y ese momento es nuestra vida entera.
There is only one moment to love, and that is our whole life.

Suddenly, as I was listening, I felt a hand squeeze my shoulder, and I heard Sixto speak the name "Yu-dea-im" at that precise moment. I looked back to see if he had approached me, but he was still standing by the projector, twenty feet behind me. So, at the end of the lecture I asked him, "Did you say the name 'Yu-dea-im' during your lecture?" He asserted that he had. "Did you come to my side and touch me on the shoulder as you said it?" He said he hadn't. "Then why did I feel that just as you spoke that name?" I asked. He looked me square in the eyes and replied calmly, "That's for you to find out," and he left it at that.

Over the next several months I began attending RAMA Mission study groups. We practiced exercises to help activate our dormant psychic abilities while learning to quiet and "order" the mind. If I were to summarize the wisdom value of these practices, it would be that all self-reflexive, conscious beings have the power to choose wholeness rather than separation and love rather than fear. These exercises emphasized mindful concentration, guided meditation, and mantralization techniques for moving beyond self-absorbed attachment to the world. They emphasized strengthening our relationship with Divine Will so that *nothing* interferes with balanced living.

Not too long after I began this work, and long before I finished the twenty-two sessions, Sixto selected me to join him on a RAMA outing with some of his most advanced students. Everyone but me who was going on that trip had received their cosmic name, which is a key to accessing the highest wisdom learned in past lives as well as a meditation tool for contact with the elder brothers. "But, Sixto,"

I questioned, "I don't have my cosmic name yet. How can I possibly accompany you on this trip? I do not feel prepared." He just looked at me. In that moment I remembered: "Yu-dea-im" was my name. I had heard it the first day I had met him. Without a word, he smiled and nodded as I spoke my cosmic name out loud. In the midst of my realization that I had long ago received this powerful, vibrational key to opening up my relationship to our star relatives, Sixto told me, "I want you to know that your companion and cosmic brother is called Ba-dea-im. Be very patient, Oscar, and at the right time, Ba-dea-im will reveal himself to you. You are destined to meet and fulfill your dharma path together on earth." After he told me that, we proceeded to go into the desert together. And on that occasion, our group achieved such vibrational coherence that the extraterrestrials joined us in physical form.

When I began disciplining the imagination and deepening mindfulness, I was told to expect great transformation. It was an awakening of higher spiritual relatedness. Once initiated into this Great Work, I felt as though I was living in some sort of fourth dimension. My sleeping, waking, and daydreams seemed to be one and the same. When I would dream things, the events in my dreams would immediately happen!

As these experiences continued, my personal transformation was bizarre. I felt that I had moved beyond interpreting these non-ordinary states as pathological, yet I desperately sought some interpretive model in which to situate these experiences. I entertained the notion that while out in the desert with Sixto, I had been taken aboard a star craft, placed in a capsule-like enclosure in suspended animation while a clone of myself remained on earth living as though it were me. Within this state of suspended animation, like Neo in the hit film *The Matrix,* I could easily experience myself being fed a vision of what was going on down below on earth. This rather fanciful interpretation made perfect sense to me and felt inherently logical. I alternated back and forth between this interpretation as a way of explaining how my reality had become so bizarre and just embracing the possibility that I had died. In that case, I imagined that I was experiencing an intermediate realm, or *bardo*, in anticipation of my next incarnation.

The Tibetan Book of the Dead talks about this. There are various *bardos* where people who have died are lovingly held until they can begin to make sense of what has happened, because death and life are experienced very much the same to a soul who is wandering between realms. Even though one is physically dead, it is common for the soul to awaken in the exact same place where the physical transition occurred, doing exactly the same thing as was happening at the moment of physical death. In cases like this, so that the soul can continue its growth and evolution beyond the mind, the external conditions of perceived reality begin to gradually lose their predictability. An example would be when someone dear to you has passed and they call you up on the phone. Maybe they even knock on your door. These occurrences are meant to gently shock you into awareness that there has been a profound change in your existence so that you realize that you have passed over.

This shape-shifting of external circumstances allows the soul to begin to understand what has happened. But unless you are already familiar with non-ordinary states of consciousness, it is natural to panic and to experience paralyzing fear. Life can become quite hellish then because when your true essence, which is love, becomes constricted, the closing down of the heart leads to even deeper descent into quite unfriendly astral realms. This is the famed purgatory, the limbo or netherworld spoken of since time immemorial by mystics and lunatics alike. Yet since this experience is all in our minds, we have the power to transform these images. As we learn to surrender our free will and embrace our experience as being ordained by Divine Will, we rapidly move from this uncertain in-between world into a realm of luminous existence, which is what we call enlightenment.

That's what this period in my life did for me. It allowed me to finally thrust through my rational mind. And when I did, I was finally granted access to the spiritual universe. Because really seeing into the true nature of creation is impossible to do without letting go of the need to know, to figure it all out. Surrendering to "not knowing" is the key to be at peace, in every cell of your being, regardless of what external realities "look like."

The first time I was able to truly embody these principles came during the last year of my apprenticeship with don Celso. To become his *segundo de mando,* or his second-in-command, he told me I would have to know what it was like to really die. So he took me to the beach one day and proceeded to have his son and son-in-law dig a grave for me in the sand. The plan was that I would be wrapped in a shroud and buried there for a little while, with a little bamboo tube to breathe through. That way I could experience what it is like to create my own inner sanctuary—my own place of respite from the human monkey-mind.

As they prepared the grave for me, I remember thinking, "This is going to be a piece of cake. All I have to do is keep a picture of heaven in my mind. With the waves rolling in the background and the way I love the beach, I'm going to be just fine. This isn't like being sent out into the desert with all the wild animals and spirits roaming all around. I'm going to have a nice little rest here. I've got this one down!"

As I lay in the grave with the wet sand being shoveled onto me, though, don Celso and his assistants started to berate me, "What an idiot," they said. "Look what he's letting us do to him." I knew don Celso was the kindest man in the world and that he would never really hurt me, and yet, their laughter made me begin to wonder. It was profoundly destabilizing. Finally, I could hear them walking away, and I was completely alone.

As I slowed my breathing and allowed myself to settle into the experience, everything was fine—for a while. I started envisioning a beautiful Crystal City, inhabited by luminous beings dressed in shimmering white vestments. And as I walked those hallways and visited the temples in that place, it felt like I had returned home. This was an unmistakably radiant celestial world of great comfort to my soul. But then I realized that none of the people I passed even acknowledged my presence. "So why aren't any of these supremely divine luminous beings acknowledging my presence? Something's not right." My expectations of how things should be just got in the way of the experience of the present moment. And with that thought, everything changed.

The minute I thought, "Something's not right," the minute I felt unwelcome in that place, I began to experience a paralyzing fear. As I struggled to relax into the present moment, I panicked. The crystalline buildings started to dissolve, to wilt like dying flowers, and fungus started growing on everything.

What had been shimmering light became grey, dark, viscous ooze. This wasn't the inner paradise that I had first experienced at all! It was then that a muffled scream began to form in my aching lungs, "Don Celso, get me out of here!" I gurgled. *No agüanto, don Celso!!* I can't take it anymore!! The panic just became unbearable. Then I lost consciousness, and I really don't remember anything until being dug out hours later.

I realized then that I still struggled to surrender to the unknown, to live the present moment. This experience revealed how self-driven and persistent I was in imposing my ego-mind upon reality. My main lesson was to diligently remain aware that strength comes from surrender. I was learning that flowing with life allows the soul to journey without hindrance and that a self-driven, willful nature must transform into open trust of the Great Mystery for growth to occur. If awakening to consciousness is a process, I was sure getting ample opportunity and exposure to it during this very difficult period of my life!

What finally brought me to a deep understanding of the need to let go was this: It was 1984 and the synchronicities were becoming unbearable. I was angry and ready to challenge the Creator's wisdom. I felt I understood the way the universe worked, and I had a lot of experience with non-ordinary reality. I felt I had learned how to access the spiritual universe. Yet I was still being manipulated by these visions that appeared to me unbidden. I was still looking for some explanation, and I was still trying to regain control. But that's not the way the universe works!

One night, I had just had it. So I went on a bender. With a bottle of *pisco* still in my hand, I got into my car. It was an orange Nissan Sentra that I had inherited from my brother

Ronald when he died. It was late at night, after curfew, when only cars with special permits were allowed on the roads. The Shining Path was blowing up electrical sub-stations in Lima, and martial law had been declared. It was really dark out—there were very few lights on in the city—and I could have been shot on sight for violating curfew, but I was crawling out of my skin with anger and despair. I just started up the car and headed down the road that connected the Lima suburb of Miraflores to the Costa Verde highway that hugged the shoreline. It was a road cut right into the 500-feet-high sandstone cliffs, which was quite treacherous to navigate. I drove frantically, gaining speed all the way down the mountain. When I reached the bottom and turned north onto the coastal highway, I floored it.

With my foot on the accelerator, I screamed out to the night sky, "Creator, whether I'm dead or alive, I need to know the truth behind this craziness. I prefer to be dead than to anguish over this continued uncertainty. If I'm really dead, I want to be *dead*." With great hubris, I threatened the One Source by vowing to take my own life. I just refused to live this life any longer. And I took my hands off the wheel and continued pushing down the accelerator.

I looked in the rearview mirror with my hands still off the wheel. As I did, I noticed that every streetlight I passed was going dark, just as I went by. *Apagón,* blackout, I remember thinking. Shining Path must have just blown up another sub-station. But it was weird how the lights would each be illuminated until I passed them, going dark as soon as I went by. Something was definitely up!

Then the car just started driving itself. I must have been doing about eighty miles an hour, and the car was twisting and turning, following every curve in the road. After a while, it started going up another dugway into the Lima suburbs on the top of the sandstone cliffs that overlook the sea. And I just started weeping. This could *not* be happening, I thought. But it was.

When the car got to the top of the cliff, it just continued driving itself through the darkened neighborhoods. Suddenly, the car swerved to the left and started heading straight toward the cliff. "Danger! Road Closed!" was printed on a sign that was supposed to serve as a road block. The car accelerated toward the barricade and the drop-off just beyond it. It's the last thing I remember seeing.

When I regained consciousness, I was still sitting in the driver's seat. I could feel blood spurting from my head where I had apparently hit the steering wheel, but I couldn't see a thing. I could hear voices, though, and I could feel someone going through my pockets, taking my wallet, and slipping my wristwatch off. I could hear them open the glove box and remove documents from there too. "He's dead alright, but hurry up, we've got to get out of here!" I heard a woman shouting then, "*Ladrones,* thieves, call the police!!!!" And I felt the human vultures scurry away; all my possessions and all identifying marks had been picked clean.

As I continued drifting back toward consciousness, I began hearing little children laughing. As I opened my eyes, I could see that the car had come to rest in a completely different neighborhood from where the road-closed sign had been. And it was bright. There was just one street, with houses on both sides. It looked like a movie set under floodlights. And there, about fifty feet beyond the car, there were these children who were tossing a big beach ball to one another. Then the laughter came again.

I started to panic. "*Carajo,* what's happening here?" I remember thinking. "What have I done?" The laughter stopped; all was silent. Then I heard a voice in my head telling me, "Take deep breaths now and just relax." It was a calming, peaceful voice. I followed the voice and began breathing and relaxing and letting go.

As I did, I could feel myself begin to leave my body. All my anxiety and my suffering just vanished. I was free. I could feel myself being drawn into a tunnel of light. I was presented with an image of my mother and father on their knees. Their grief was overwhelming. Then I saw my infant daughter, living with her mother, growing up without me. Then I was shown the most sublime heavenly realm where the bliss was just ecstatic, and the closer I would let myself go to that place, the more it was like paradise. I was free of everything. No constriction, no anxiety, no craziness. I was in the heart of love, of the Creator. And then I realized that it was a choice.

The minute I allowed myself to consider the suffering of my daughter and others in my life who still needed me, I was back in my body again. The pain I felt was so excruciating, I can't even describe it. My mind felt dull and my heart heavy. "Breathe deeply, now get up and get out of the car," I heard the calming voice in my head again. I obeyed.

When I got out of the car, I could see that it was completely totaled. As I looked into the distance, I saw a cocky-looking Peruvian guy with a full head of slicked-back hair, a black leather jacket with an STP® patch on the lapel. He looked like he had just come off a racetrack, and he wore dark glasses. He began sauntering toward me. I could hear him speaking telepathically, using street-smart Lima-lingo, "You know what's happening, don't you?" he asked simply. "I'm dead, right?" I replied. "Of course you're dead," he responded. "You are a being of light, and we are waiting for you on the other side. But you're also on earth, and your human community also needs you. It's your choice. I need to ask you some questions first, though, in order to determine what serves your soul's progression the most. We want to be able to get you to the right place."

I was nervous. I sensed that I was being given a choice about what *bardo* I could hang out in, and I could feel my anxiety rising. Plus, I was still concerned that I might just be a total, raving psychotic. I mean, here was the equivalent of the Egyptian Ibis-headed Thoth recording my life history in order to determine my eternal fate, and he was showing up to me as a Peruvian version of a macho–cool dude, a race car driver complete with an STP® logo on his black leather jacket. This was totally nuts! Especially since I really disliked anything to do with motor sports!

As I stood there, I became aware of the children playing and laughing again. I began rejoicing in their play, and as I did, their laughter was louder than before. They started throwing the ball again, closer now to where I stood. Then my self-doubt and my self-loathing kicked in, and I remember thinking, "They're laughing *at* me because I'm such an idiot." As soon as that thought materialized, they stopped laughing. They stopped playing. They stopped throwing the ball. I realized then that if I opened my heart and surrendered to the beauty of the moment, if I could just rejoice in the joy they were feeling, *that* was my reality. It was in that moment when I realized that we all have the power to change our reality by shifting our perception and reframing the way we think.

Realizing this, my tears flowed freely out of gratitude for the gift of the children's playfulness. As I opened my heart to this deep gratitude and peace of the moment, they passed me the ball, inviting me to join them in their play.

Then the leather-jacket wearing emissary from between the worlds began asking me questions. "I see that you have been fascinated with the occult from a very young age. I want to know what you think about the possibility that God exists. Do you feel that God has a place in your life?" he asked me. "Not really," I replied, "I'm in this worrisome predicament precisely because He hasn't answered my insistent calling. At this moment, I feel disconnected from God. Instead, for me, God is an energy that fills the universe." He told me then, "Well it's fine that you feel that way. Every feeling has a place in this life and in the life to which you are being called." I sensed he was making sure that I really understood that there is no separation between Creator and Created.

Then he asked about my conception of God. He asked what I felt was most "godlike" in myself. He asked if it was possible that I could be at peace in any moment, and in any world or state of consciousness, and most important, free of any self-serving attachment to a God. As he did, I knew he was giving me the opportunity to deeply understand that I share in the impersonal ineffability of the I AM without needing to be a separate "self." Whether I am alive or dead, whether I am caught in time or floating in the a-temporal realm, it makes no difference because it is all part of the universal continuum of being. Above/below, within/without, here/nowhere, we are all passersby within the great cosmic ocean.

I settled into a deep inner peace in realizing that I chose love and wholeness over fear and separation. As I relaxed into this deeper kind of Knowing he said, *Hijo, entra a tu carro y empieza a respirar profundamente. Cierra los ojos y cumple el mandato que tienes en tu ser.* My son, get back into your car, and begin to breathe deeply. Close your eyes and carry out the work you came here to do.

As soon as I sat back in the car, I heard the woman who had called the police. She was standing with them now, lamenting as they pulled me out of the car. "He's dead, oh my God, he's dead," she wailed. I had no pulse. I was cold as ice. I was dead. They threw a sheet over me, lifted me into the back of a pick-up truck, and took me to the police station, where they laid me out in an empty room.

I have no idea how much time passed, but I felt heat coming into my body once again. The blood flow from toes to head was restored. I remember taking this deep breath of air and feeling my body. I stretched a little, sat up, and the sheet fell away. I could see everyone in the room was aghast. *Como es que está vivo? No tenía pulso! Estaba muerto!* "How is he alive? He didn't have a pulse! He was dead!" they stuttered. "How can I be dead," I shouted back. "I was just reborn!" And that's exactly how I felt. Everything was new. I felt anointed with the understanding that what issues forth from me shall *be* the world in which I live. By choosing to allow the blessings and the perfection of the present moment to guide my life, my once disquieting monkey-mind was finally at peace.

Further Teachings

In the journey toward consciousness, our greatest ally in the process of burning away the dross of ego is deep attention to the *present moment*. As we open ourselves, becoming more aware and present in each moment, we align with and we attune to Source—we connect.

In this task, the Pachakuti Mesa Tradition can help us. This is because it embodies and reflects the cycles, pulses, and rhythms of the natural world, which are most fully appreciated as we come into the present and as we open to these—in *every* perfect, present moment. As the Zen master Wu Men so beautifully summarized it, "Ten thousand flowers in spring, the moon in autumn, a cool breeze in summer, snow in winter. If your mind isn't clouded by unnecessary things, this is the best season of your life." As we begin to engage in this Great Work, living in harmony with the natural order, ceremonially aligning to the pulses, rhythms, and cycles of our sacred earth, our purpose as earthbound souls is revealed.

Every life-form within the great sacred hoop embodies patterns and behaviors, structures and actions that unfold in ways that are orderly, prescribed, and completely harmonious. The spiral unfolding of a nautilus shell, the opening of a fern, the dance of honeybees, the progression of the sun through the sky, and the slow movement of the sunflower that follows the sun's path are just a few examples of these patterns and behaviors. These orderly patterns, movements, and creative impulses are a natural part of life—and they are expressions of the aesthetic beauty that is the *art* of living. Ritual and ceremony, which are the terms we humans give to this graceful unfolding, is everywhere reflected in these rhythms, pulses, and cycles.

As we begin to pay close attention to these rituals of nature—when we begin living our lives inspired by the beauty within creation—these graceful structures and actions begin to inform our behavior. We find ourselves tuning in to the present moment more frequently and modeling our lives according to what we observe. We find ourselves living the Blessing Way, as the Navajo express it.

We use the Pachakuti Mesa to intentionally magnify these moments of deep alignment and mindful presence as we enact earth-honoring rituals that *mirror* these natural rhythms and pulses. This is what our ancestors did as they performed graceful rituals of reverence for nature befitting seven generations. These are ceremonies that honored the solstices and equinoxes, the cycles of the moon and the changing seasons that were ubiquitous among earth's original peoples.

Celebrating these events—just as our ancestors did—reminds us of what we can change in our lives and what we can't. When we allow nature to inform our actions as we harmonize our lives and honor these moments of convergence between earth and sky, we come into alignment with higher and deeper levels of being. We bridge the above and the below—becoming *part* of the beauty that we witness and the ritual cycles that we reflect. We walk the path of the hierophant, which is the bridge between "as above, so below" drawing sacred power from above in service to the below. As we do these things, we learn to use ordinary life for coming into real life; for coming back into alignment with our greater purpose, which is to be *present* in each perfect moment and to be thus aligned with the Source of Creation itself.

As we connect with Source through the graceful rituals we enact with the help of our Pachakuti Mesa*s*, we are living as did the ancient ones. They knew that nature informs purpose. As they configured their rituals and their ceremonial spaces to mimic and mirror the beauty and grace of creation, they were able to restore harmony in their own lives, remembering what matters and freeing themselves of impulses, desires, and instincts that lead to chaotic conditions. As we choose to be inspired by the perfection of the present moment, to observe the graceful rituals of nature with patience and precision, to discern what we can change and what we can't, and to align ourselves with higher and deeper levels of being, we *become* masters of our thought, our intention, and our will.

By surrendering to the perfection of the present moment, we reclaim freedom. By practicing mindfulness, we silence the chatter of dis-harmonious thoughts that keep us from experiencing the beauty both within and around us. As we look to nature to model our actions, we reclaim our power to co-create a more harmonious world. Having awakened a conscious relationship with the Divine Will, we are no longer subject to the tyranny of lower thought forms or emotions. We have awakened the higher mind.

The consciousness that we cultivate as we deeply *connect* to the beauty all around us is open to everything that comes through. We do not silence or reject any emotion, fear, or lower impulse. We simply observe it. This is consciousness that requires a letting go of all attachments to everything that we thought we were—the abandoned child, the fearful protégé, the insecure professional, the angry victim. All insecurities, self-loathing, judgment, attachment, aversion, and *need* recede from view when we align ourselves with the beauty of the present moment and simply *allow*. This illumined-mind consciousness is that which is willing to dive deep into the liquid universe and just let go, flowing and moving gracefully with the changing cycles and rhythms and seasons and pulses of creation.

Enacting graceful rituals with the help of our Pachakuti Mesa helps us to come into that space of awareness and awakening to the beauty of *what is*. When we do these things, we calm our anxieties and our worries, realizing that we are going to be fine with whatever is coming through. By remembering to first cultivate gratitude for the beauty of the natural world and to just accept the love and the joy in every perfect moment, without attachment, we become a truly open vessel for projecting love into the world. And, when we engage in these ritual practices, all that is beyond ourselves begins to mirror the calm, the peace and the harmony that we feel within ourselves.

Practices for Transforming Mind: Connecting with Our Purpose and Power

Quieting the Chatter of the Ego-Mind

In previous chapters you have learned how to *commune* with all the powers and forces of the universe, to *consecrate* yourselves and the ground upon which you construct your Pachakuti Mesa altar, and to artfully *compose* graceful, earth-honoring rituals invoking and harmonizing the forces and powers residing in *Pachamama, Mamakilla, Wiracocha, Inti,* and *K'uychi* that are contained in the south, west, north, east, and center portions of your respective mesas. In this practice, you will call upon these forces and powers to guide and support you as you learn to quiet the chatter of the ego-mind and awaken to the beauty of an illumined, *higher* mind, whose intentions are perfectly aligned with an infinitely loving, universal consciousness.

To begin, sit quietly at your Pachakuti Mesa and begin the "Communing with All That Is" practice that you learned in chapter 1. Extend your hands in front of you, palms-up toward the heavens to assist you in this process. Consciously empty yourself of any needs, desires, or limitations as you continue to breathe deeply, through the nose, with the tip of your tongue in gentle contact with your upper palate. Picture all worries and cares flowing effortlessly out through the soles of your feet and the palms of your hands. Now rotate your hands so your palms are directed toward the earth as you continue to draw in the golden shaft of light through your crown, bathing every cell of your body in light and love. Take as long as you need to really *feel* yourself become as a hollow bone and a clear channel for the manifestation of spirit on the earth.

Next, reflect for a moment on the powers you called into each direction piece at the close of chapter 3, bringing the wisdom and beauty of each of these into your awareness. To more fully embrace the wisdom of these powers so these may assist you in your cleansing and awakening, turn your hands toward the center of your altar and consciously call these powers into your medicine ground again. Then tone their names, as you did in the practice at the close of the last chapter, three times each, beginning in the south, with *Pachamama,* then moving to the west, to tone *Mamakilla,* then moving to the north and toning *Wiracocha,* then to the east, where you will tone *Inti,* and finally, moving to the center and toning *K'uychi,* just as you learned to do in chapter 3. After you finish, pause and feel, with gratitude, the shift in consciousness and the awakening that comes as you engage in this ritual process.

In this way, you activate the Pachakuti Mesa. Upon completion of these steps, light the candle that sits in the east of your mesa.

Once you have completed activation of your mesa, begin to visualize a glowing, golden orb of light about six inches above your crown. Picture that this orb of light is emitting pristine waves of light energy down and through your crown, gently cleansing and feeding every cell and corpuscle of your body. This is your higher mind, the one that is *above* your seventh chakra. Its energy is what you bring into yourself as your visualize this beautiful orb of light.

If you like, you can gaze softly at the lit candle in the east of your mesa as you do this. As you engage in this practice, open again to the truth that all is mental and that with the power of our awakened higher mind, we are able with pure heart and intention to heal and create all conditions in the material world.

All is Mind: Awakening to
the Healing Power of Intention

For this exercise, you will need a pendulum, preferably a pyramidal-shaped pendulum that is made of lead. If you have ever used a pendulum before as a diagnostic tool, please forget all that you learned about that process. In this practice, the pendulum is used to *heal* with the power of the mind.

To begin, place the pendulum in your dominant hand and place your other hand, palm facing up, just under the pendulum. Calling forth the power of your mind, will the pendulum to swing in a forward and backward direction. This is the motion that is associated in the Pachakuti Mesa Tradition with re-balancing the spiritual body. Next, will the pendulum to stop and then to begin swinging in a left-to-right fashion. This is the motion associated with re-balancing the physical body. Next, still the pendulum with your mind and begin to will it to swing in a counter-clockwise fashion. This is the motion associated with re-balancing the emotional body. As you still the pendulum again, will it to swing in a clockwise fashion. This is the motion associated with re-balancing the mental body. Finally, still the pendulum so that it remains motionless over your hand. This still-point energy is that which is associated with the healing eternity of the soul body.

After you have practiced these movements, pick up each of the directional pieces of your mesa, one by one, in both hands. As you lovingly hold these pieces, with the power of your imagination, picture your own image within the piece. The *Pachamama* crystal or stone holds the energies to all physical healing. The *Mamakilla* shell or bowl of water holds the energy of emotional healing. The *Wiracocha* feather holds the energy of spiritual healing. The *Inti* candle holds the energy of mental healing. The *misarumi* holds the energy of your soul's evolution on the planet. Know, as you gently place your own image within these pieces, that you can extend and retract this at will. By placing your image there, you are simply invoking the powers of the associated directional pieces to assist in your process of rebalancing. Replace these pieces on your mesa.

Next, think of a condition that you would like to balance in yourself. Is it physical, emotional, spiritual, mental, or does it have an energetic signature more akin to your soul than to these other aspects of yourself? If you are unsure which area of yourself is most fully being called into action in this moment, there is no need to worry. The higher mind is infinitely wiser than you think, and there is no way to do this practice "wrong."

Retrieve the pendulum in your dominant hand and allow it to swing effortlessly above the piece that you have chosen to represent the condition you would like to transform. Don't will it to swing at all, but just let it do its thing. Most likely, it will swing according to the motions outlined above: backward and forward for spiritual rebalancing, left and right for physical rebalancing, etc. But if it doesn't, don't worry. Again, the higher mind knows what it is doing, and it knows what you need. Your task during this practice is simply to imagine yourself perfect, balanced, and healed. Think of the condition that you want to balance. View yourself with peace, serenity in your eyes, with love in your heart, with balance in your being. That is you now. Mentally create that image of yourself in perfect balance, and *so it is*. Practice this on a daily basis for whatever condition you need to bring into balance.

CHAPTER 5

HEALING BODY / THE ART OF COOPERATING WITH ALL-THAT-IS

The physical body is effect, responding to energy and consciousness as cause. Healing always points to a renewal of creative powers, toward a condition that is vital, stirring, strong, and whole, as befits a creative beginning.

The Challenge of Healing Body: How Can We Really Heal Ourselves and Our Beloved Planet Using the Pachakuti Mesa?

She purses her lips as she wills herself to stand, but her limbs buckle and refuse her command. "Damn stroke has ruined my life!" she moans, as she flops back into the chair. "How did I end up this way?" she obsesses. "Is there a reason I must endure such torturous physical disability for the rest of my life?"

As Pachakuti Mesa carriers, we recognize that the body is much more than physical form alone. As Rumi tells it, "The body's a mirror of heaven," and self, nature, culture, world, and cosmos are completely intertwined. *Everything* that exists in the universe has vibration and frequency. It is *all* energy, and energy creates *all* form. From the light of spirit and consciousness to mind and then into matter, spirit literally projects through thought into the third dimension. As the physicist David Bohm once said, "All matter is frozen light." These vibrations of light and consciousness ultimately inform all manifested reality.

Thus, whether our focus is on healing the physical, social, or the planetary body, the path to transformation is also the same. All healing transformation requires first that we come into alignment with the higher vibrational frequencies of spirit. To do this, we engage soul, spirit, heart, and mind as discussed in previous chapters. We commune and consecrate and compose and connect to detect and direct the finer forces of energies and vibrational radiations that are beyond audible sound and on either side of the visible light spectrum. Because the body's innate healing ability is the direct result of the mani-festation of spirit within it, to heal we must first attune.

As we do, we remember our inherent *wholeness* as our birthright and as our true essence. We align the frequencies of gross matter within our human form to the higher frequen-cies that we were created to mirror. You see, the Divine that we carry within us patterns *all* molecular structure, from the farthest reach of the stars to each cell within our physical bod-ies. By attuning to the at-One-ment we spoke of in the last chapter, we enter again into sacred relationship with the hoop of life. And as we align again with this knowing, we recog-nize our interdependent relationship with all seen and unseen dimensions of *Pachamama's* web.

Most "modern" religions emphasize earthly *transcendence* as a key to positive transformation, yet the wisdom traditions practiced by our ancestors and embodied in the Pachakuti Mesa provide for a very sensual and *earthly* experience. With our rituals, we envision and imagine the sounds, smells, look, and feel of the rich earth, the flowing water, the singing wind, the creative flame, and the sacred rainbow that bridges the worlds. We do this with such discipline, compassion, and clarity that these powers cannot but help to "show up" in eager anticipation to serve *us* with gratitude and love.

As we construct our altars, we celebrate *relationship* and re-claim deep *connection* with ourselves, our communities, and our beloved *Pachamama*. As we call forth the power of nature into our altars, we recognize that we are *not* isolated or alone. The construction of our altars helps us to realize that we are luminous strands within the whole. Through our altars, we recognize ourselves as spirit *embodied*. We cry tears of gratitude as we celebrate our presence and our full participation in the physical world.

In my almost thirty years of teaching this tradition, I have found that most people who come to my workshops and trainings are looking for a change. They realize that everything that they have accumulated and felt a sense of ownership of is no longer cutting the mustard. So, initially, they come for self-healing. Little by little, however, they move from a focus on healing the self to a focus on healing relationships with one another, on reclaiming a sense of belonging and community, and on restoring right relationship with our beloved Earth mother. That is why these native traditions are so relevant to the suffering of the modern world.

The art of creating sacred community, of focusing on the sacred reciprocity of *ayni* and service expresses the nature of God/Goddess Creator Spirit, which is love. This focus wakes us from the fantasy of unconscious desire and projection. It encourages right action, borne of compassionate spiritual wisdom, which unites. But we can only succeed in this agenda if we are able to hold this vision of oneness in front of us always. To do this, we need to come together as like-minded individuals who are bonded by a greater purpose. As Gary Snyder summarized it, at the end of his powerful poem, "For the Children," we need to "stay together, learn the flowers, [and] go light!"

The Pachakuti Mesa Tradition and the Creation of Sacred Community

In Lima, life was increasingly difficult. Revolutionary extremists were creating chaos as counter-insurgency forces struggled to maintain control of the city. In December of 1985, to commemorate their leader's birthday, Shining Path bombed ten banks, a shopping center, a judicial office, and eight electrical towers. As a result, residents suffered through electrical blackouts almost every day. The soaring inflation and hoarding of durable goods by merchants made it difficult to find even the basics in stores. We were standing in bread lines while gunfights were erupting in the streets! I was anxious to provide my daughter and myself with a life of greater opportunity and less danger to life and limb. I yearned to go back to the United States.

It was the spring of 1986, and don Benito had just made his earthly transition. My daughter's maternal grandparents were moving to Florida to live in a retirement community. They had been kind enough to allow my daughter and her emotionally unstable mother to live with them until the completion of my two-year fellowship work obligation in Peru. I missed my little girl terribly. I knew she missed me too: I had *seen* how much she needed me during my near-death experience at the end of 1984.

So, with great relief in my heart, I traveled to Durham, North Carolina, to pick up Andrea and to settle with her in Carrollton, Georgia. It was the fall of 1986. I took a part-time faculty position in the psychology department at the University of West Georgia. My full-time work consisted of heading up the Spanish department, teaching World and Social Sciences, and coaching the women's varsity soccer team at a private school to offset the cost of Andrea's tuition.

As if that wasn't enough, on the evenings when I didn't have class, I began to hold RAMA study group sessions in my home. After our trip to meet the RAMA guides in the desert, don Sixto had asked me to become the southeastern coordinator of RAMA study groups in the United States. I also had a handful of psychotherapy clients I would see on Saturdays. My days and evenings were full!

At the university, I shared my small office with some very interesting personalities. My office mate was Raymond Moody, whose book *Life after Life* had made him the premier authority in the world on the topic of near-death experiences. Our conversations gave me a language for talking about my own experience in new ways. Bill Roll, a parapsychology expert, occupied the office next door. He was famous for his poltergeist studies and for investigating paranormal activities of all kinds. Since I was so familiar with the "unseen" world of shamanic allies, working on psi projects with Bill was a logical next step for my own re-entry into the world of Western sensibilities. I was learning, through these experiences, to translate my shamanic experiences in new ways. I was being prepared to fulfill my promise to don Celso to take his teachings "to the North." I was being completely supported by the unseen world every step of the way. Later that fall, I opened my mesa for the first time to a U.S. audience.

Because of its prominence in transpersonal and humanistic psychology, the department at West Georgia would host monthly grand-rounds where specialists in gestalt, bioenergetic healing, psi research, and other emerging modalities would be invited from all over the country to speak. I had been working with some graduate students who were interested in how to integrate shamanism practices into their psychotherapy practices. As a result of the incredible feedback they were providing, Mike Arons, who was the chair of the department and who had been Maslow's colleague at Brandeis, asked me to present at one of those grand-round events. So I began preparing to present all the shamanic wisdoms I had learned over the previous seventeen years.

Since I was very young, I have always had the ability to see associations and relationships among disparate things. I see how everything is interconnected and whole. Even as a young child, I felt this innate need to reveal the unmanifest integrity of the big picture.

Through my apprenticeship with don Celso and then with don Benito, I recognized the similarities between the practice of a north coastal *mesada* and the ceremonial earth offerings, or *haywas,* of the Southern Andes where don Benito was from. I was entranced by the correspondences between these two traditions and the teachings of the RAMA Mission too. And then there were the traditions of Western Mystery Schools that I had immersed myself in along the way.

I knew I was destined to carry the traditions of my homeland to the North. I wanted to bring something to the world that would transform the way psychotherapy was practiced too. And, I knew whatever I presented needed to resonate with a more community-based life style that people were yearning to reconnect to in their lives.

I realized that what was missing was a unifying vision. I started to deeply study the Inka cosmo-vision and its depiction on a golden plaque that had once graced the walls of their most sacred temple in Cusco, the Qorikancha. It was a pure-gold plate that was melted into gold bullion by the Spaniards when they conquered Peru. But an early historian named Juan Santa Cruz Pachakuti Yamqui had drawn it from memory in all its beauty. The organizing principles of this cosmology stuck with me as I thought how to integrate all that I had learned.

So as I prepared to present these materials to my teachers and colleagues at West Georgia, I just configured all of what was coming into my consciousness into a pattern, and there it was! I knew in that instant that the Pachakuti Mesa was about to be born. And I knew it would be an *open-ended* field of creative possibility that brings grace and beauty and healing into the world because of the way it integrates all these sources and practices.

As I thought about how to present it, though, I realized that these psychology professors and scholars were not going to want to experience ritual. They were going to want to understand *concepts.* So I grappled with just how to articulate the healing wisdom of the Peruvian *curandero's* mesa in terms of Jungian psychology and Maslow's model of self-actualization and Gestalt therapy to the professors who had trained me who were also the founders of this Third Force in psychology.

When I walked into the room that night to present the mesa, the auditorium- style seating, the cinder-block walls, and the glaring fluorescent lights were overpowering. "I'm going to need time to set this up," I realized, as my heart started pounding in my chest. But I centered myself, communing deeply with my prayers and then consecrating the space. The minute I made my offerings of breath and fragrant waters and song, the minute I woke up the field, I knew that this was the vision that don Celso had accessed. He had seen into the future and into this moment. It was the reason he had entrusted me with the task of "bringing it North."

In that moment, my nervousness vanished. I thought to myself, "My teacher has seen me doing this, so I know it's all going to be okay. This is what I have been prepared for. Everything is going to function just as it has been foreseen."

When everyone came into the room and got settled for the evening's presentation, I could see it was a completely full house. Now it was time to begin. But the neon lights were really bothering me. As I looked around the room at my professors, my colleagues, my students, and everyone else who was present, I froze. I thought to myself, "Who am I, where am I, am I dreaming?" And the only thing that came to me was this: "Fraser," I said to one of my graduate students, "please, I just can't stand these neon lights. Please, turn them off." He flipped the switch, and it went completely dark. It was a new moon in Carrollton, Georgia, that night.

The moment the lights went out, all of my shamanic allies showed up. Everyone who had ever been present with me in the rituals I had done with don Celso was there. I could feel them all patting me on the back and assuring me they were there to support me. So I started to sing my songs, I started to do my rituals. I forgot all about giving the audience any interpretive framework at all. I just started doing my thing, activating the fields of the mesa, and making my offerings. I began working the mesa as though the altar itself was a patient, doing all the ritual processes that don Celso had taught me. I really got into my prayers and as I did, the place started to light up. My *vista* started to kick in, and the room became as bright as day.

As I looked there into my mesa, I saw Professor James Klee, a giant of a man who had revolutionized the field of psychology by introducing systems theory into the study of personality. He had been one of my main advisors. And he was present in the audience that night.

I could tell he was having some problems. "Dr. Klee," I heard myself saying, "would you please come up and stand in front of my mesa?" I got my staffs and my rattles out. I called on the support of all my shamanic allies while holding an intention of robust health for this beautiful man. I made my offerings and began raising the vibration as I rattled. I began pulling things out of him, strengthening his human "container" to receive a new energetic template, and then began to invoke the presence of spirit within matter to bring him back into balance with his wholeness. As I worked, there was not one sound in the room.

When I was done, I asked simply, "How are you feeling?" "Fine, Oscar, thank you," he replied simply. When he took his seat, though, the auric radiance around him was like that of a ten-year-old child rather than that of a seventy-year-old man. And so I knew that something big had happened. He had experienced a profound transformation for sure.

After that, I asked for some floor lamps to help illuminate the space, and I called everyone up to form a circle around the mesa. I first began teaching about the pre-verbal awareness that is characteristic of shamanic perception. It is the type of knowing that is born of the senses. It is instinctual, much like that of any creature who is sensitive to the ways of Mother Nature. As we connect deeply to this feeling while praying for its presence within our Pachakuti Mesas, we access unlimited healing powers.

I shared how everything that exists in the universe has its own characteristic wavelength, or frequency of vibration, whether it is a star that is light-years away, a cell in your body, or a thought and image inside your head. Our physical body is integrated with and directed by these higher frequency energy fields. By tapping into these, light and consciousness are grounded in substance. Working with the Pachakuti Mesa while raising the vibration and holding impeccable intention makes new realities manifest on earth.

As I spoke, everything just started to pour out. Remember that I had never before articulated how the Pachakuti Mesa is a system for healing. But as I spoke in that moment, everything became embedded in me as it poured through. I explained the ceremonial protocol, the Pachakuti Mesa etiquette that we practice right now as though it had always been present. And I knew that I had a psycho-spiritual transformational practice on my hands that could reach people from any culture. I explained the entire cosmo-vision that had come to me, and then I had the audience tone the directions of the mesa for the first time ever. And then I asked them to sit back down.

I returned to my place in front of the mesa, and I scanned the group with my *vista*. "Are there any questions," I asked?

After a moment of silence, Mike Arons spoke. He had received his doctorate from the Sorbonne based on his ground-breaking research on the psychology of creativity.

"Oscar, have you ever done this before with a group like this?" he asked me. "No, this is the first time, Mike," I replied. "You know that I've been in circles with Fritz Perls, with Virginia Satir, and many other luminaries of group therapy," he continued. "I have studied with all of these major therapists, yet I've never experienced such an effective way of bringing about emotional consensus and 'common-ground' psychological clarity as tonight. You know that restoring relationship is a key to healing on all levels. That's what group psychotherapy is about. And that's what you've been doing in this room since you began your presentation tonight. You are onto something, young man, and I want you to be teaching this practice in your psychology classes from now on." And they allowed me to teach the first course on the psychology of shamanism at the university the next term.

During the next few years, I continued to teach at West Georgia, and I began offering seminars on the Pachakuti Mesa throughout the southeast. As I did, I realized how the actual ritual and beauty of the mesa, with its emphasis on sacred reciprocity, could provide a safe space for healing all forms of wounding. The Pachakuti Mesa was creating a transformative space for disaffected individuals to heal. As these group processes unfolded, anchored by the power and the beauty of the mesa, people were moved from a place of isolation and disconnection to a place of cooperating with and providing service to the whole. They were moving from a place of being "victims" to a place as "volunteers" in the creation of a new reality, founded on the principles of sacred reciprocity.

They were receiving healing as they were giving gratitude to all the powers of nature that are embodied in the cosmology of the mesa. The Pachakuti Mesa was having a deeper collective, social impact. It was establishing a healing state for the abused, wounded, marginalized, and ostracized. It was healing a social need, bringing a breath of fresh air to an otherwise very constricted society. I began teaching how to honor the earth in earnest.

During our weekends together, while sitting and standing in a circle around the Pachakuti Mesa, we would tone the directions and call in the forces and powers of the universe. With our rituals of transformation and healing, we practiced Trusting Soul, Honoring Spirit, Opening Heart, Transforming Mind, and Healing Body. The power and beauty of the Pachakuti Mesa Tradition that was emerging was apparent.

As part of the trainings that I offered, I began teaching these groups how to construct earth-offerings as don Benito had shown me. We went on pilgrimages to sacred sites where we would offer the *despachos* we created. We also began building *apachetas*.

These stone cairns or mounds, which are found throughout South America, infuse a place with refined energy as they tap into to the energy grid of the Mother. By creating and nurturing *apachetas*, we expand and enhance *Pachamama's* luminous web. We renew ourselves as we connect with those pulsing energies while adding our own unique and powerful energies to the web. *Apachetas* carry our burdens and restore us to the flow of sacred living again.

After our weekends together, these groups were continuing their work. They were doing pilgrimages to sacred sites and making earth-offerings. They were beginning to form sacred communities. And as they did, they were healing body and opening to wholeness again.

The Ayllu as Sacred Body in Balance

Ayllu is a Quechua term that refers to this understanding of sacred community. Ayllu-mates (who are called *ayllukuna* in Quechua) are united by a common focus, which is to care for and cultivate sacred relationship with the landscape upon which they live. Creation stories, common ancestors, mountain lords, or other reminders of emergence and belonging unite *ayllukuna* in purpose and service, as offerings are made to these, in a spirit of gratitude and sacred reciprocity.

In the Pachakuti Mesa Tradition, our shared visionary focus is to harness the power of creation from spirit, as did our ancestral peoples, and to properly channel it so that it serves the entire Earth community. This occurs as we compose and participate in graceful earth-honoring rituals, either at natural places of power (Bear Butte in Wyoming and Uluru in Australia come immediately to mind) or at built sites like the Great Pyramids in Egypt, the megalithic temple complex at Stonehenge, and the mind-boggling subterranean passageways at Chavín de Huantar (which I described in chapter 3). These are all places where our collective earth-offerings transmit vital life force and gratitude to renew us. Like batteries, they are repositories and storehouses of sacred power that are periodically *charged* by the sacred communities who tend them so they can continue to nurture the health, good fortune, and vitality of these *ayllukuna*.

So in the lineage of the Pachakuti Mesa Tradition, *ayllus* are groups of people who are aware of their interdependent wholeness. As luminous strands in the grand weaving that is life, *ayllus* provide a safe, cooperative, loving, and earth-honoring environment. As Pachakuti Mesa Tradition *ayllukuna*, people from all walks of life can find sanctuary from the isolation imposed by modern techno-industrial living.

Social-change movements frequently fail because they don't pay enough attention to nurturing people's inner lives. This is important so that we can maintain hope no matter what is apparently happening around us. Our Pachakuti Mesa communities allow the type of respectful and non-judgmental self-exploration that leads to a well-nurtured inner life. This is possible because heartfelt participation in sacred communal ceremonies helps us to grow new eyes and ears with which to see and hear the ancient wisdom stories which nature has to tell through us. By fostering a direct experience of our own divinity through reverence for the living soul of our beloved Mother Earth, we provide a much-needed respite from the outer craving for control and approval that is fueled by the illusion of material security that most of us were born into.

Our *ayllus* help to sustain sacred relationship. As we come together to perform graceful rituals and celebrate our common connections to the landscape, to one another, and to our birthright as reflections of the one Source, we heal. Healing body is, therefore, all about sacred relationship. It is about the rituals and the songs. It is about reestablishing communities and connection. And the Pachakuti Mesa becomes a fulcrum for creating and maintaining these sacred communities because it provides the ground and the glue for containing and safely channeling these energies of creation.

Thus, the fifth "C" in our story is that of *cooperation*. As we *commune* with our soul's purpose, we align. As we *consecrate* our lives to spirit, we surrender to All-That-Is. As we *compose* graceful rituals, we bow in respect to all our relations. As we *connect* deeply with the Source within, we discover our purpose and power. And as we *cooperate* with one another, we act as servants to the greater whole. This is the *love* that structures our lives. Awakening to this truth allows us to heal.

Many of us are looking for answers to life's meaning and are hoping to locate someone or a group that can satisfy that thirst. No one individual or group can satisfy all of the desires in and of themselves, for that is the role played by the soul of each individual. However, what we can do as Pachakuti Mesa carrier *ayllukuna* is to aid in lighting the way for each other as we seek our way out of the darkness. As we continue to "re-member" ourselves as a shamanic global family, we co-create the New Earth from this expanded awareness. We emerge into the luminous One Source that is our true essence. This is the way of the future. It is the way of new birth!

Practices for Healing Body:
Cooperating in Service to Life

The Wednesday Night Link-Up

Each Wednesday night, Pachakuti Mesa carriers from all over the world gather together energetically to celebrate and strengthen our growing shamanic community. Link-ups generally occur between seven and ten P.M. and feature the Pachakuti Mesa of the host (or a communal mesa that represents the entire *ayllu*) as the anchor for the evening's activities. It is helpful to bring a sacred item from your own mesa to include on the mesa to physically anchor your energetic participation.

The purpose of the Wednesday link-up is to link our mesas in order to add the intention of each of us to a single concentrated intention of global power for the cleansing and healing of *Pachamama* as well as the collective psyche. Link-ups can be practiced individually, as we sit at our own Pachakuti Mesas, collectively, as described above, or by simply connecting our awareness and highest heart, wherever we are, at this sacred time.

To begin, stand to the south of your mesa (or in a circle around the central mesa that is serving as an anchor) opening your crown, your brow, the nape of your neck, and your heart center. Open to the *saiwa,* which is a golden column of light energy that streams down from the heavens. Direct this energy through the palms of your hands to the center of your mesa. Open your *qosqo*, which is your navel, and feel yourself connected by an umbilical cord of energy to the center of the mesa. Express your intention to heal our beloved Earth and all her children. It should now be 9:45 P.M.

Beginning at 9:45 P.M., simply allow energy to flow through you into your mesa and deep into *Pachamama*, feeling your connection with the others in other parts of the world who are also in this practice. After fifteen minutes channeling this energy, you may feel a shift in consciousness, but don't worry if you don't. Once you have made your energy offering via the Pachakuti Mesa to our beloved Earth mother, you may choose to use the heightened energy to do healing on yourself, or others, to share personal wisdoms, to honor the seasons, or to engage in any other reverent celebrations of life. If a personal healing is to occur, it is helpful to have community members who are receiving these energies lie in the south (with their heads toward the center of the mesa). All present direct loving energies toward the receiver, who simply opens her crown to receive the blessings of the mesa. Other healing modalities such as Reiki, Sound Healing, or Energetic Touch may be incorporated here at the discretion of participants.

When you are complete, close the mesa by directing your palms to the center of the mesa and tone the directions one time each. Then, with your hands still facing the center, take a deep breath and blow your gratitude into the central ground.

The Wednesday night link-up is often accompanied by sharing food and fellowship with one another. This is a wonderful opportunity to deepen our connections and to enact the cooperative living that the Pachakuti Mesa Tradition celebrates.

Despacho Haywas (Offerings)

The reverent creation and ritual offering of a *despacho* gives each of us the chance to step into the sacred center of our own life with deep gratitude and prayers for our world. When you make a *despacho*, you prepare a delicious meal for the unseen world—it is as if you cooked and served a holiday dinner for your family and your friends while adding love and prayers along with each of the main ingredients and the spices.

You can create a *despacho* using items from nature that you find here rather than using only the "traditional" items that are available in the Andes. These ingredients may come from the grocery store or from the woods or beach near your own home. Wherever you live, you are still able to add an essential ingredient to each item that you place in the *despacho*—your heartfelt gratitude for the many gifts you have received and your prayers for the healing of our beloved planet.

Physically, a *despacho* is composed of items called *recados*, which are infused with prayers and ceremonially arranged in a beautiful pattern on a large piece of white paper. The mandala-like creation is folded into a bundle and ritually offered to the fire or to the earth. These *recados* are associated with each of the directions, representing different kinds of offerings, according to the "tastes" of the tutelaries that are associated with each direction. Animal products feed the *Tirakuna*, who are the watcher spirits in the south. Plant products are offered to the *Auquis*, who are the nature spirits of the west. Mineral products like sand and crystal serve the *Malquis*, who are the spirits of the great trees of the north. Creations we make with our own hands are offered to the *Machula Aulanchis*. These are the Benevolent Old Ones of the east who love beautiful things that humans create. A shell, a cross, and *untu* (llama fat) are placed in the center as special gifts to the *apu* guardians of all the directions.

Each of the items you place in the *despacho* are expressions of your gratitude for the corresponding blessings in your life. Examples include sugar, candy, sprinkles, or raisins, symbolizing the sweetness of life, red and white flower petals for love and compassion, seeds and grains for abundant harvests, animal cookies for the blessings of your four-legged friends, gold and silver foil for the sun and moon, beads or glitter for the stars, cotton for clouds, colored string for the rainbow, which is the bridge between worlds and the integration of all that is.

As you create the *despacho* in an atmosphere of reverence, connect your loving intentions with the prayers of people throughout the Andes as well as with people in varied cultures in other parts of the world where similar offerings are a part of daily life.

While you create the *despacho*, medicine songs or music are offered to raise the vibration and accompany the process. First, lay out the paper and the offering items in the west of the mesa. Have each person present circle the mesa clockwise, select an item, and take it back to his/her seat. Then have him/her hold the item in his/her right hand and gently breathe a prayer into it. When the ceremonial leader directs, each person circles back to the west and places the item onto the *despacho* paper in a way that creates a beautiful and balanced arrangement of the whole.

After all the items have been beautifully laid out on the paper, the paper is folded carefully to contain the arrangement. After folding the paper, the pattern of the design no longer exists in the physical form—yet the feeling of the design remains in your minds and is held in the energies all around you, even after you bundle and wrap the *despacho*. Secure the bundle as you tie yarn around it, just as you would any gift. Then sprinkle it with Florida Water or an alcoholic beverage and wrap the *despacho* in a ceremonial cloth (which will be removed before the offering is placed in the fire or in the earth). The *paqo,* or ceremonial leader, then prays over the ritual bundle and may ask that each participant breathe in a final prayer to help energize the completed *despacho*.

Most commonly, a *despacho* is offered to the fire and burned, or it may be offered to the earth. Someone prepares

the fire or digs a hole in the earth ahead of time. The fire or the ground is fed with cornmeal, tobacco, coca leaves (or bay leaves, here in the U.S.) and is given a libation of alcohol or

Florida Water. Medicine songs and music may be offered at this time to deepen the feeling of sharing sacred space.

When the time feels right, go with the *despacho* to the place where the offering will be presented (for example, the east of the fire) and form a circle with all participants. Then unwrap the fabric from around the bundle. Reverently place the *despacho* in the fire (to send its prayers through the rising smoke) or in the earth (to plant its intention, like planting a seed in the ground). Continue to hold space until you feel that it is time to close the circle, either when the offering has been completely consumed by the fire or when you intuitively know that the ceremony is complete.

Remember, you are creating beauty through the art of the *despacho* as you say, "Thank you!" and return a small part of the many gifts you have received back to the Source. Thus, it is fitting to take pleasure in each step along the way. To make and offer a *despacho* is a form of sacred play as you select and offer your ceremonial medicine to the world.

Building and Tending an Apacheta

Building an *apacheta* brings people together in reverent, prayerful ceremony to remember our relationships with all life through prayerful offerings of gratitude. Physically, *apachetas* are piles of rocks, or cairns, found throughout the Andes that mark the high points of mountain passes from whence all water flows downward, nurturing the landscape. Yet much more than this, *apachetas* are understood as guardians and teachers, as powerful allies and relatives. Like the *apus,* which their graceful stone structure mirrors, they channel energy from the heavens into our beloved Mother Earth.

In the Pachakuti Mesa Tradition, we build *apachetas* as "acupuncture" points that strengthen the flow of energy running throughout the earth by means of our offerings and our prayers. In addition, building an *apacheta* provides opportunities for us to unburden ourselves as we transfer our troubles into the stones that we leave on these earth altars. Our "seed thoughts" of healing intention are made manifest by our purity of heart, our deep compassion, and our care. We tend and feed *apechetas* with *haywas* of cornmeal, tobacco, coca leaves, fragrant waters, and more. Because we also receive as we give, *apachetas* are also places we may journey to as pilgrims to tap into the renewing energy of *Pachamama's* energetic grid.

An *apacheta* may be built by a single individual or a group. There may be a single group intention that guides the process, although individuals in the group often create our own intentions as well. Common intentions for creating *apachetas* include building and strengthening *ayllus*, learning to live in a state of gratitude and grace, committing to walk more softly on the landscape, and awakening compassion in the world.

In the Pachakuti Mesa Tradition, *apachetas* typically have twelve foundation stones, symbolizing the twelve sacred *apus* that don Benito most frequently prayed with, as well as a stone in the center that serves as an anchor. These are supplemented by other stones, often brought by community members from faraway places, to link *ayllus* together energetically.

To create an *apacheta*, first center yourself and align with all who are present to create a single body and common purpose. Standing in a circle together, practicing the alignment techniques presented at the close of chapter 1 while holding hands is a good way to proceed. Then consecrate the ground as you did when creating your Pachakuti Mesa. Offer a few drops of Florida Water to open sacred space, draw a circle with blue cornmeal, an equilateral cross with tobacco, and place a perfect, three-leaf *kintu* in the center.

On the consecrated ground, lay the base of the *apacheta*. Select five substantial stones to include a stone for each of the cardinal directions and one for the center. Imbue each stone with the energies of *Pachamama, Mamakilla, Wiracocha, Inti,* and *K'uychi*, respectively. Next, select two stones to place in the southeast, the northwest, the northeast, and the southwest, respectively. These twelve *apu* stones, plus the anchor in the middle, complete the circle. Once the base is formed, other stones are added, intuitively placing these according to where each stone "wants" to go. If many community members are participating, encourage each to bring stones to add to the altar. The top of an *apacheta* (called the *ushnu*) is built to be flat in order to accommodate offerings made by passing journeyers or by those caring for it. The *apacheta* is intended to evolve over time, to reflect the additions of beauty that are offered.

When you construct an *apacheta*, you are committing to tend it as well. Over time, an *apacheta* will change its form. Wind and water, earth-tremors and passersby may all contribute to this change. These changes are not accidental but point to energy shifts that can be read. When approaching or caring for an *apacheta*, it is important to do so in a state of awareness and receptivity. The *apacheta* will communicate with you what it needs.

When you have constructed an *apacheta*, and when you return to tend it, you will nourish the spirits and spiritual connection it provides. Common offerings are water, Florida Water, cornmeal, tobacco, sage, flowers, incense, feathers, and more. Remember to gently blow, or *phukuy*, your prayers into the material objects that will carry these, just as don Benito taught me to do. Remember, *haywa* offerings are about honoring and remembering your relationship with each spirit in material form.

Caring for an *apacheta* often means reassembling and adding stone energy, as well as clearing old debris. Often, items from your mesa will call to you to be offered to an *apacheta*. Since these are already infused with all the love and attention of your sacred altar, the energy these add to the *apacheta* can be very helpful, for healing the whole. When you have completed the process of constructing or feeding the *apacheta*, call in the directions by toning just as you do when you open your Pachakuti Mesa. Remember also that there is no "right" or "wrong" way to give offerings. The most important thing is to always trust and follow your heart.

EPILOGUE

The Courage of THOTH,
Which Is The Heart of the Healer

*The longest voyage you will ever take is the seventeen inches from your head
to your heart. When you resist, this takes lifetimes. When you surrender,
you are already home.*

The Challenge of Courage: How Can We
Embrace Courage in Our Own Lives?

"Who am I? Why am I here? What is the meaning of life?"
For thousands of years, we have all wrestled with these basic
questions of being. In this year of 2013, prophesied by so
many peoples as the time of great turning, which precedes
new beginnings, our quest for the answers to these fundamental questions is more urgent than ever. On our quest to
understand ourselves as humans, to seek answers to the basic
questions of our purpose, we are carried forward in our reflections by both the anxiety and the hope of our yearning for
truth. "How can I make a difference? What power do I have
to change the world? How can I reclaim a sense of deep connection even when I feel so disconnected and alone?"

This quest to recover what we already know; to remember
who we are as powerful, whole, and at-one with the Great

Originating Mystery takes courage. It is a voyage that takes all who engage it from head to heart in order to rediscover our true nature. This is the original definition of *courage,* which shares the same word root as "heart." Courage is about embracing and rejoicing in every moment, and trusting that we have all that we need. It is about remembering that we are already whole. The teachings and tools of the Pachakuti Mesa can help us to *re-member.* Trusting Soul, Honoring Spirit, Opening Heart, Transforming Mind, and Healing Body— these are tools that we can all use, every step of the way. As we learn to commune with our soul's journey, to consecrate ourselves to the Great Spirit within us, to compose rituals that restore us to sacred relationship, to connect with the power of our higher mind, and to cooperate in service to the whole, we reclaim our birthright: We are powerful beyond measure, co-creators of material worlds.

As we work the fields of the Pachakuti Mesa, we spiral ever inward toward ourselves. And as we do, we realize that consciousness begets matter, language begets reality, ritual begets relationship, nature begets purpose, and love begets life. As we move in a clockwise direction around the Pachakuti Mesa, we learn the ways of *Llankay* in the south. This is the Quechua term for right action, industriousness, and diligent work. Then, we become aligned with *Munay* in the west: the place of the heart, the emotional body, and unlimited, compassionate love and feeling. Moving to the north, we encounter *Yuyay,* which is our sacred re-membering, our awareness of spirit. In the east is *Yachay,* which is wisdom and a knowing beyond the intellect. And in the center, we are aligned with *Huñuy,* a seamless flow of purposeful living that unites the many to the one. So as we work the fields of the mesa in a clockwise fashion, we move from the body as right action to the heart as compassionate feeling to the spirit to the mind to the center where the soul unifies everything. Thus, the Pachakuti Mesa itself provides the template that brings us back into sacred relationship. As we align with these energies we are transformed. As we act from this place of deep reverence and compassion, spiritual re-membering, and higher mind, we reclaim our birthright as stewards for one another and for our beloved planet. Right action, borne of compassionate spiritual wisdom, unites. These are the wisdoms of our ancestors. They are the teachings my life has revealed.

Remember this always. The Great Work is not so much about changing the world as it is about changing ourselves in the process. As we commit to this quest, and the graceful honoring of all life that will naturally flow from our actions, positive transformation must occur in the world. To unlock the magic of personal healing and global transformation, the Pachakuti Mesa can support us. We need only to act from a place of sentient awareness of the I AM.

Your journey is sacred and a blessing. I am infinitely grateful for the immortality of the soul that has brought us to this moment, together. As you carry this sacred bequest forward, I salute you. For when I gaze upon you, I see the future of humanity. I see a bright future for *Pachamama's* Seven Generations whom we have been entrusted to protect. I thank you humbly for your service, and I am grateful you have found your way here. May your path be blessed with beauty and love.

I am Oscar Manuel Miro-Quesada, your brother and servant. And it is in sacred and peaceful relationship that I so remain.

One More Practice: Looking in the Mirror and Learning to See Yourself

For this practice, find a small hand mirror and integrate it into your Pachakuti Mesa. After centering yourself, pick up the mirror in both hands and gaze deeply into it. Look first with the left eye and then with the right. Notice the difference as you continue to gaze gently and lovingly at your reflection. See the Divinity that looks back as you gaze. You are the same. You are not the same. You are Creator. You are Created. You are cause and effect and the paradox that is both contained and resolved in this opposition. You are without and within, above and below, the circle and the self. You are the vibration and the flow.

When you have reflected on these wisdoms, place your image within the mirror and release it to its sacred purpose. Then turn your mirror toward your Pachakuti Mesa. Know yourself as divine and that the mirror image of yourself that is reflected into the mesa is how all healing works.

When you are complete, simply pause and feel. Give gratitude for all that you are.

APPENDIX

The Heart of the Healer Foundation (THOTH) was founded in 2001 with the mission of "preserving indigenous wisdoms and restoring our earth." As a vehicle for reawakening modern society to the ancient wisdoms discussed in this text, THOTH is a gathering force for personal and planetary transformation. A visit to its website (*www.heartofthehealer.org*) will provide the reader with links to valuable information about how to deepen in apprenticeship to the Pachakuti Mesa Tradition.

Options listed on the website include links to previously recorded interviews with don Oscar, advance notice of upcoming webinars, information about don Oscar's teaching/apprenticeship schedule, as well as links to THOTH-Endorsed Teachers who offer trainings in the Pachakuti Mesa Tradition in multiple locations around the country. As noted on the website, "*The Pachakuti Mesa Tradition: Cross-Cultural Shamanic Arts for Personal and Planetary Renewal* is a five-part series of intensives that aligns the traditional teachings of Peru and the wisdom of its heritage with the needs of the present day. Providing a comprehensive foundation and profound initiation through ceremony and prayer into the living heart and soul of the Pachakuti Mesa Tradition, this apprenticeship series will help participants cultivate a deeper relationship with nature and the unseen world and receive multiple opportunities for self-exploration, empowerment, and profound personal growth. This powerful program is open to all people who desire to be of service to themselves, their families, their community, and Mother Earth, whether they are long-time mesa carriers or new to this tradition through personal and communal ceremony."

In addition, the THOTH website provides portals for visitors to enter into dialogue with members of our global shamanic community through participation in community-wide blogs. The Heart of the Healer also has an active presence on Facebook and YouTube.

For more information about don Oscar's teaching and apprenticeship schedule, as well as registration information for upcoming workshops and sacred journeys/shamanic travel programs, please also visit *www.mesaworks.com.*

ABOUT THE AUTHORS

 DON OSCAR MIRO-QUESADA originated the Pachakuti Mesa Tradition of cross-cultural shamanism (PMT), and is the visionary founder of The Heart of the Healer (THOTH) Foundation. He is a respected *kamasqa curandero* and *altomisayoq* adept from Peru, OAS Fellow in Ethnopsychology, Invited Observer to the UN Permanent Forum on Indigenous Issues, and member of the Birth 2012 Welcoming Committee convened by Barbara Marx Hubbard. Don Oscar has been leading shamanic apprenticeship expeditions to sacred sites around the world since 1986, with special emphasis on the millennial healing traditions of Peru and Bolivia. A popular teacher at numerous U.S. educational centers, his work and programs have been featured on CNN, Univision, A&E, and the Discovery Channel. His life is passionately dedicated to the revitalization of ethno-spiritual wisdom traditions as a way to restore sacred trust between humankind and the natural world. For more about don Oscar and information about how to participate in this work, please visit *www.mesaworks.com* and *www.heartofthehealer.org*.

BONNIE GLASS-COFFIN, Ph.D., is an internationally recognized professor of anthropology at Utah State University. She has studied with Peruvian *curanderos* since 1982 and is author of *The Gift of Life: Female Spirituality and Healing in Northern Peru* as well as numerous scholarly and popular articles on the topics of shamanism and transformation. She began apprenticing with don Oscar in 2005, experiencing the transformative power of these wisdom teachings and integrating these deeply into her life. This deep apprenticeship has enabled her to take a leading role in presenting don Oscar's life-work to a wide audience. She is an endorsed teacher of the Pachakuti Mesa and an avid practitioner of earth-honoring traditions in her home community of Logan, Utah. For more information about her work, please visit *bonnieglasscoffin.com* or visit *anthropology.usu.edu.*

Jesusgate: A History of Concealment Unraveled
by Ernie Bringas

Messiah's Handbook: Reminders for the Advanced Soul
by Richard Bach

Blue Sky, White Clouds
by Eliezer Sobel

Inner Vegas: Creating Miracles, Abundance, and Health
by Joe Gallenberger, Ph.D.

Flames and Smoke Visible
by Danny Lliteras

What To Do When You're Dead
by Sondra Sneed

Your Soul Remembers: Accessing Your Past Lives through Soul Writing
by Joanne DiMaggio

When the Horses Whisper: The Wisdom of Wise and Sentient Beings
by Rosalyn W. Berne, Ph.D.

Rainbow Ridge Books publishes spiritual, metaphysical,
and self-help titles, and is distributed by Square One
Publishers in Garden City Park, New York.

To contact authors and editors, peruse our titles, and
see submission guidelines, please visit our website at
www.rainbowridgebooks.com.

For orders and catalogs, please call toll-free:
(877) 900-BOOK

RELATED TITLES

If you enjoyed *Lessons in Courage*, you may also enjoy other
Rainbow Ridge titles. Read more about them at
www.rainbowridgebooks.com.

The Divine Mother Speaks: The Healing of the Human Heart
by Rashmi Khilnani

The Buddha Speaks: To the Buddha Nature Within
by Rashmi Khilnani

The Cosmic Internet: Explanations from the Other Side
by Frank DeMarco

Conversations with Jesus: An Intimate Journey
by Alexis Eldridge

Conversations with Jesus, Book 2: An Invitation to Dance
by Alexis Eldridge

Dance of the Electric Hummingbird
by Patricia Walker

Coming Full Circle: Ancient Teachings for a Modern World
by Lynn Andrews

*Afterlife Conversations with Hemingway: A Dialogue on
His Life, His Work and the Myth*
by Frank DeMarco

*Consciousness: Bridging the Gap Between Conventional Science and
the New Super Science of Quantum Mechanics*
by Eva Herr